T0155669

Inclusive Design for a Digital World

Designing with Accessibility in Mind

Regine M. Gilbert
Foreword by Ron Rateau

Apress®

Inclusive Design for a Digital World: Designing with Accessibility in Mind

Regine M. Gilbert
New York, NY, USA

ISBN-13 (pbk): 978-1-4842-5015-0   ISBN-13 (electronic): 978-1-4842-5016-7
https://doi.org/10.1007/978-1-4842-5016-7

Managing Director, Apress Media LLC: Welmoed Spahr
Acquisitions Editor: Natalie
Development Editor: James Markham
Coordinating Editor: Jessica Vakili

Distributed to the book trade worldwide by Springer Science+Business Media New York, 233 Spring Street, 6th Floor, New York, NY 10013. Phone 1-800-SPRINGER, fax (201) 348-4505, e-mail orders-ny@springer-sbm.com, or visit www.springeronline.com. Apress Media, LLC is a California LLC and the sole member (owner) is Springer Science + Business Media Finance Inc (SSBM Finance Inc). SSBM Finance Inc is a **Delaware** corporation.

For information on translations, please e-mail rights@apress.com, or visit http://www.apress.com/rights-permissions.

Apress titles may be purchased in bulk for academic, corporate, or promotional use. eBook versions and licenses are also available for most titles. For more information, reference our Print and eBook Bulk Sales web page at http://www.apress.com/bulk-sales.

Any source code or other supplementary material referenced by the author in this book is available to readers on GitHub via the book's product page, located at www.apress.com/978-1-4842-5015-0. For more detailed information, please visit http://www.apress.com/source-code.

Printed on acid-free paper

I dedicate this book to my daddy Allen Gilbert, Jr. - he told me I could do whatever I put my mind to and he was right. Thank you to all of my students, who have taught me more than I could have ever taught you.

To all my friends and family: you all have been with me on my journey - thank you!

Table of Contents

TABLE OF CONTENTS

About the Author

Regine M. Gilbert is a user experience designer, educator, and international public speaker with over 10 years of experience working in the technology arena. Her passion for accessibility stems from growing up with family who were disabled. Since working in technology, she has spearheaded accessibility initiatives within the organizations in which she worked including creation of guidelines and training. She has a strong belief in making the world a more accessible place—one that starts and ends with the user.

Regine is a Visiting Industry Assistant Professor at NYU Tandon School of Engineering, teaching User Experience Design to students in the Integrated Digital Media Program. In addition, she has previously taught the part-time User Experience Design course at General Assembly. Some of the organizations Regine has had the pleasure of working with include Disney, JP Morgan, Four Seasons Hotels and Resorts, Ralph Lauren, Columbia University, and Vitamin Shoppe. She is a Certified Accessibility Professional through the International Association of Accesibility Professionals.

Acknowledgments

When I started to think about why I wrote this book and who I would like to acknowledge, the list is long. So I will start at the beginning of my lifelong journey of learning about accessibility and different disabilities.

Growing up, I had a mother with a cognitive disability and a cousin who was deaf. I never thought of them as different, and I learned a little sign language along the way. Thank you, mama Mary Anne Gilbert and cousin Tammy Holmes.

My family has been supportive every step of the way, and I want to thank my three brothers, Allen, Corey, and Reggie, and my sister-in-law Winnie for all their help and support along the way. My partner in life Jorge Junior Mena Sivira, thank you for your patience.

When I got involved with digital accessibility, I learned a lot from the founders of the a11y NYC Meetup: Shawn Lauriat, Thomas Logan, and Cameron Cundiff. They bring together great guest speakers on a monthly basis and I have been able to learn so much from them.

Some of the best teachers have been people I have and have not met in real life. To those in the disability community, thank you for your tireless efforts in promoting a more inclusive world. To those I continue to learn from: Catherin Kudlick, Liz Jackson, Debra Ruh, Chancey Fleet, Clair Kearney-Volper, Neil Millikin, Kat Holmes, Matt May, Amy Hurst, Allen Goldstein, Tatiana Mac, Svetlana Kouznetsova, Jennison Asuncion, Damien Senger, Karwai Pun, Eric Bailey, E.J. Mason, Joe Devon, Lindsey Kopacz, Tae'lur Alexis, Erin Newby, Anne-Laure Fayard, Nefrititi Matos, Sarah Horton, Whitney Quesenbery, and Reggie Bennett.

To those that inspire me on a daily basis: Maurice Cherry, Jonathan Soffer, Luke Dubois, Tega Brain, Carla Gannis, Elton Kwok, Eric Maiello, Jenelle Woodrup, Jhanele Gree, Michael Bernard, Ife oluwa Lawal,

ACKNOWLEDGMENTS

Scott Fitzgerald, Elizabeth Henaff, Kathleen Sullivan, Kathleen McDermott, Justin Hendrix, Jay Leibowitz, Alexis Seeley, Janice Brown, Adaora Udoji, Michael Rain, Mich Lyon, Maya Brooks, Christy Crawford, Dara Sanderson, Quiessence Phillips, Bill Curtis-Davidson, Jose Zambrano, Stacy Smith, Benedetta Piantella, Nicholas Gustin, Mark Skwarek, Daniel Krasner, Kyra Peralte, Corey Malone, Tanasha Lawcock, Eric Talbert, Steven Thrasher, Galina Tsypin, Andrew Clark, Christina Morrillo, Tanya Valle, Willie Morales, Elliot Carlisle, Mich Weston, Christophe Drayton, Megan Innes, James Vanie, Ronald Ondeyko, Marsha Cooper, Sacha Seraydarian, Jarrad Henderson, Heather O'Neill, Elle Elliot, Ramon Guillemard-Torres, Binh Ngyuen, Ariba Jahan, Keith Franco, Jessica Santana, Evin Robinson, Ren Vasey, Shawn Vasandani, Jan Baker, Sela Lewis, Chad Schroer, Courtney Wiggins, Belinda Johnson Tiffany Linzan, Felicia Grey, TeLisa Daughtry, Steve Chartier, CJ Dillon, Susan Zweig, Ryan Snelson, Jocelyn Miller, Claudio Romano, Nitya Narasimhan, Jordan Green, Dian Holton, Paul Anthony Webb, Antoinette Carrol, Phim Her, Kojo Boateng, Joe Formica, Maurice Franklin, Krya Peralte, Christine Wong Yap, Elizabeth Travelslight, Kamilah Cole, Angela Fludd, The Collective, and Robert Salley.

Without you I would not be where I am today: Karl Hudson Phillips, Elise Braun, Gerald Glackin, Janis Yost, Nathan McDonald, Madeline Koren, DeAngela Duff, Touseef Mirza, Aaron Neeley, Angelica Moreno, Barbara Jackson, Jewel Taylor, Karen Hipsher, Lanette Hauck, Kamil Bir, Yuto Navarette, John Angel, Annica Nolan, Erin Hawke, Maria Rapetskaya, Michel Kekerovic, Cyril Lagarde, James Angel, Lair Paulsen, Jarrod Lawrence, and Deon Lambert.

Most grateful to the publishing team at Apress who gave me this opportunity and worked with me. Thank you, Natalie Pao, Jessica Vakill, and James Markham for your time and efforts and for all your hard work.

Foreword By Ron Rateau

As an expert in the field of accessibility, having worked with end users, product owners, developers, brand managers, stakeholders, and everyone in between from public sector to private sector for nearly 20 years, I have heard the term accessibility used in a variety of ways but rarely are the comments from a place of "enthusiasm" with statements like

- *Accessibility—that's not our problem.*

- *Wait, what—how much is it going to cost us to make this site accessible?*

- *Lawsuit for an inaccessible image? It's free to surf the Web.*

- *Making the site accessible will mess up the aesthetics.*

With *Inclusive Design for a Digital World*, Regine has made the idea of accessibility and design a seamless process that can be implemented at the early design phase by addressing design requirements from the start.

My first introduction to Regine was when I attended one of her UX/UI Series in New York City about the impact of stakeholders' roles on accessible design in their market. She leveraged her experience as a designer and what she had learned from the challenges she faced in her work. Regine brought up key points about background images to color contrasts used on "call to action" buttons. She highlighted that if a designer checked for compliance by reading up on the W3C recommendations, they would get a laundry list of 12 guidelines and 61 success criteria (not to mention 17 added SC in WCAG 2.1). She stated that she recognized that this seemingly complicated list is too robust for a designer to simply follow along for corrections. This prompted two guests, who were UX designers in the audience, to have a lively exchange regarding what is considered compliant vs. best practices. She shared her insights on the Web Content Accessibility Guidelines 2.0 (WCAG 2.0) Level AA as a reference point, but explained to the attendees that their roles as designers should be specific to what their industry were trying to achieve.

I understand some of the perceived challenges that designers face when thinking about how to make a web site accessible as well as be in line with WCAG 2.0 ruleset. However, what I empathize with more is the experience of the actual user when trying to navigate a web site that has not been designed with accessibility in mind.

I remember in 2005, I was tasked to train a classroom of blind users on how to navigate a government web site on desktops. We spent 2 days trying to figure out an alternative way to complete an online form because the screen readers were unable to announce labels for each text field. At that time, my role was to simply walk through a web page. That immediately turned into a hands-on, interactive experience. I found myself walking up and down the aisle to each user leaning in so they can whisper to me what labels they were unable to hear due to the sensitive information they were required to type. At the end of this session, the class just wanted a telephone number to call when they got home, so if they had any issues, they could ask a family member to help. This was a problem that unfortunately many people with disabilities were accustomed to. They were not able to have the same quick, easy, and simple interaction with the online forms like a sighted person would.

Fast-forward to 2019 and 15 years later, we are still facing similar issues with user experience. It is why Regine's book is even more relevant and necessary today. With more and more of the average person's life being spent online on various devices, from laptops to mobile phones, her approach to breaking down designers' way of critically thinking about accessibility challenges during the design phase will help to ensure compliance and usability for all.

Not only will Regine's book give seasoned designers what they need to know when it comes to accessibility being implemented in their design but her years in classrooms teaching young talented individuals has proven she is an advocate for people with disabilities.

I don't need easy. I just need possible.

—Bethany Hamilton

Introduction

Have you ever been left out of something? Have you ever wanted to get into a place that didn't allow you in? How did that make you feel?

> *Life may not be fair, but that doesn't give you any excuse not to be.*
>
> —Elizabeth Jackson

Upon attending my first A11yNYC meetup in New York, I met a person who was blind, and as many conversations go, they asked me what I did for a living. I mentioned I was a UX designer and help make web sites more usable. She asked me, "Do the companies and people you work with ever think about people like me?" At the time, I had worked on a few freelance projects and had not heard anyone mention accessibility.

After a long pause, I answered, "No," and proceeded to say that I will make sure that we do think about it in whatever work I do. She had posed a question to me that forever changed my perspective on the things I work on.

Thinking back on the question first asked, we know what it feels to be left out of something. When we create products and experiences that are not inclusive and accessible, there is the possibility we are leaving folks with the feeling of being left out of experiences.

This book provides a foundation for making more inclusive and accessible experiences through case studies and hands-on exercises.

Who Is This Book for?

This book is meant to be a starting point and reference guide for those who are new to accessibility or have an interest in knowing more about accessibility and how to incorporate more inclusive practice into their day-to-day work.

As a consultant and educator, I have found that a lot of people are not clear on what accessibility is or why it is important. For many, it is a new area. I took a lot of the questions I have been asked over the years and created the outline of the book.

> *Creating a culture of accessibility inclusion is about making sure everyone who works on, delivers or uses your services or products can access them.*
>
> —Julianna Rowsell

How to Use the Book

The book is divided into ten chapters and an appendix with additional resources. We learn by doing, and throughout the book, there are opportunities to try things for yourself so you are able to get a better understanding of accessibility.

> **Chapter 1,** "Designing with Accessibility in Mind," discusses accessible digital design and models of disability.

> **Chapter 2,** "Best Practice for Web," discusses information architecture and content strategy and provides a high-level overview of accessible HTML, CSS, JavaScript, and ARIA.

Chapter 3, "If It's Annoying, It's Probably Not Accessible," provides examples of inaccessible products and relation to web content accessibility guidelines.

Chapter 4, "Web Standards," reviews accessibility guidelines from across the globe as well as providing high-level explanation of the web content accessibility guidelines.

Chapter 5, "Design Principles," covers a couple of different design strategies and frameworks for creating a more inclusive and accessible experience.

Chapter 6, "Inclusive Design Research," discusses research methodologies and planning, and recruitment of people with disabilities.

Chapter 7, "Assistive Technologies," highlights a selected group of assistive technologies and provides a case study of the Microsoft Adaptive Controller.

Chapter 8, "Planning and Implementing Inclusive Designs," covers creating a culture of accessibility, design systems, and implementation of accessibility.

Chapter 9, "Usability Testing," includes the "hows" of usability testing, test plan example, and BBC case study.

Chapter 10, "Beyond the Web," discusses past accessible innovations and the future of accessibility with augmented and virtual realities.

The Appendix contains information on additional resources related to accessibility and inclusive design.

INTRODUCTION

Throughout this book, there are references to real case studies as well as some practical frameworks that can be applied to the creation of digital products. There are many references throughout the book and they are not meant to provide a one-size-fits-all solution, because when it comes to accessibility and inclusive experiences, context needs to be taken into consideration. In all instances when dealing with accessibility, it is best to bring in an accessibility professional, working with people with disabilities by participatory/co-design, or get the training for your team. We all have to start somewhere, and this is a good place to be.

Design is oftentimes the starting point and this is where the book begins, with designing with disability in mind.

Let's get started!

CHAPTER 1

Designing with Accessibility in Mind

How we got here...Where we are...Where we are going

The 21st century has provided us with more connectivity than our ancestors could have dreamed of. From the emergence of the iPhone to voice technology, most of us do not go a single day without interacting with a digital device of some kind.

Throughout this book, we will look at designing with accessibility in mind for the digital age. Examining some practices related to code, design principles, user research, usability testing, planning and implementation, and what a more accessible future might look like.

This book takes the approach of looking at the user experiences. As a user experience designer, my focus is on being an advocate for the user and making sure the product is fitting the needs of the user.

In recent years, there has been more of an emphasis on making products more accessible and inclusive. But what does it mean to design inclusive and accessible experiences? You could ask five different people and they would give you five different responses.

My personal definition is that people either feel good using a product or they don't.

© Regine M. Gilbert 2019
R. M. Gilbert, *Inclusive Design for a Digital World*,
https://doi.org/10.1007/978-1-4842-5016-7_1

Imagine if 90% of the web sites or mobile apps you use today locked you out. Everyone else continues to experience the convenience of mobile banking, the connectedness of social media, and the freedom of online shopping, but, for you, they're inaccessible.

For the 57 million people with disabilities in the United States, this is their everyday experience. People with visual, auditory, motor, speech, and cognitive disabilities rely on various assistive technologies and alternate methods of interaction to use digital documents and web and mobile apps.

People with visual disabilities may rely on screen readers, braille displays, zoom functions, or high contrast colors to get value from what's displayed on screen. People with auditory disabilities often rely on captions or transcripts for video content. People with motor disabilities might require speech-to-text software or keyboard-only interactions. People with speech disabilities require a nonvocal means of interaction. And, finally, people with cognitive disabilities often require thoughtful and organized layouts with clear direction.[1]

For the purpose of this book, we will use Webster's Dictionary to define accessibility. It is defined as follows:

> *Easily used or accessed by people with disabilities: adapted for use by people with disabilities.*

Often times, accessibility is viewed as a series of checkboxes to complete; it doesn't have to be that way. Accessibility is not only about compliance, it is also about usability. We first need to look at our potential users. Who will be using your product? Think about ALL of your potential users and who they could be.

As Kat Holmes said, "Design is much more likely to be the source of exclusion than inclusion."

---

[1]What is digital accessibility? Deque www.youtube.com/channel/
UCvNQ5aJllZ50i49jtMKebOQ

When addressing accessibility, we need to keep in mind the areas accessibility focuses on:

- Visual: Blindness, low vision, color blindness

- Hearing: Deaf and hard of hearing

- Motor: Inability to use a mouse, slow response time, limited motor control

- Cognitive: Learning disabilities, distractability, inability to focus on large amounts of information

The social model of disability is utilized in this book. The social model of disability says that disability is caused by the way society is organized, rather than by a person's impairment or difference. It looks at ways of removing barriers that restrict life choices for disabled people. When barriers are removed, disabled people can be independent and equal in society, with choice and control over their own lives.

Disabled people developed the social model of disability because the traditional medical model did not explain their personal experience of disability or help to develop more inclusive ways of living.

(An impairment is defined as the limitation of a person's physical, mental, or sensory function on a long-term basis.)

Changing Attitudes to Disabled People

Barriers are not just physical. Attitudes found in society, based on prejudice or stereotype (also called disablism), also disable people from having equal opportunities to be part of society.

Medical/Social Model of Disability

The social model of disability says that disability is caused by the way society is organized. The medical model of disability says that people are disabled by their impairments or differences.

Under the medical model, these impairments or differences should be "fixed" or changed by medical and other treatments, even when the impairment or difference does not cause pain or illness.

The medical model looks at what is "wrong" with the person and not what the person needs. It creates low expectations and leads to people losing independence, choice, and control in their own lives.

Social model of disability, some examples are as follows:

- A wheelchair user wants to get into a building with a step at the entrance. Under a social model solution, a ramp would be added to the entrance so that the wheelchair user is free to go into the building immediately. Using the medical model, there are very few solutions to help wheelchair users to climb stairs, which excludes them from many essential and leisure activities.

- A teenager with a learning difficulty wants to work toward living independently in their own home but is unsure how to pay the rent. Under the social model, the person would be supported so that they are enabled to pay rent and live in their own home. Under a medical model, the young person might be expected to live in a communal home.

- A child with a visual impairment wants to read the latest best-selling book to chat about with their sighted friends. Under the medical model, there are very few solutions, but a social model solution ensures full text audio recordings are available when the book

was first published. This means children with visual
impairments can join in with cultural activities on an
equal basis with everyone else.[2]

In the subsequent chapters, we will discuss these areas of accessibility
in more detail and some of the assistive technologies used in order to
facilitate digital experiences for people with disabilities.

Some of the areas we will cover in this book include the standards
used for accessibility set forth by the Web Accessibility Initiative (WAI)
in Chapter 2. If you find something annoying with digital experiences, it
is not accessible; there are cases discussed in Chapter 3. There will be an
overview on web content accessibility guidelines 2.0 and 2.1 as well as the
internalization of accessibility in Chapter 4.

In Chapter 5, we will look at frameworks and personas that can be
utilized. One way to approach a project is to apply the W5H approach for
design and development of your products. This could be an important first
step into creating more Inclusive Designs. W5H stands for

- **Who**: Who is using your product?

- **What**: What are they doing?

- **Where**: Where are they doing it?

- **When**: When are they doing it?

- **Why**: Why are they doing it?

- **How**: How are they doing it?

W5H

Examining the W5H can be helpful after an idea has been brought
forth and before it is built. Often times an idea for a product is created
without much thought when it comes to the users of the product and, in

---

[2]The social model of disability vs. medical model www.disabilitynottinghamshire.
org.uk/about/social-model-vs-medical-model-of-disability/

particular, people with disabilities. Keep in mind in the 21st century people are quick to respond if your product does not work for them.

There are major corporations working on getting knowledge about accessibility out to the public. Microsoft has taken a particular interest in the area of Inclusive Design, and they created an Inclusive Design toolkit which looks at people who may have permanent, temporary, or situational disabilities. This is a great example of incorporating design thinking and the W5H, as shown in Figure 1-1. More information related to user research will be discussed in Chapter 6.

One arm

Arm injury

Different people benefit

By designing for someone with a permanent disability, someone with a situational limitation can also benefit. For example, a device designed for a person who has one arm could be used just as effectively by a person with a temporary wrist injury or a new parent holding an infant. We call this the Persona Spectrum.

Figure 1-1. *Microsoft Inclusive Design toolkit showing permanent disability (person with one arm), temporary disability (person with an arm injury), and situational limitations (person holding a baby in one arm)* www.microsoft.com/design/

Inclusive Design means making your product available to as many users as possible. Technology is a part of life and as such, we no longer go a day without it. Many people have a role in the design of technology and we are all creators. Chapter 7 will show some case studies related to different types of digital experiences such as web, mobile, and emerging technologies like augmented reality.

As an adjunct professor, I get the pleasure of teaching students about user experience (UX) design. Whether you are planning for a lesson or the launch of a new product, you will need to consider planning and implementation. In Chapter 8, we will get into detail about creating a more inclusive culture and what to plan for.

There are several methodologies used in order to facilitate learning such as Universal Design for Learning (UDL; Figure 1-2 shows what UDL is and is not), and for creation of products, one may use user-centered design or design thinking.

UDL is...	UDL is not...
✓ A way to optimize teaching to effectively instruct a diverse group of learners.	⊗ A curriculum or technology platform.
✓ Based on insights from the science of how people learn.	⊗ One method of teaching all students. A variety of methods are used to give all students an equal opportunity to succeed.
✓ Flexible in how students access material, engage with it and show what they know.	⊗ An "us" vs. "them" resource. UDL benefits all kids, not just those who struggle.

Figure 1-2.   *What UDL is and is not*

UDL is 'A way to optimize teaching to effectively instruct a diverse group of learners.' 'Based on insights from the science of how people learn.' 'Flexible in how students access material, engage with it and show what they know.' UDL is not... 'A curriculum or technology platform.' 'One method of teaching all students. A variety of methods are used to give all students an equal opportunity to succeed.' 'An "us" vs. "them" resources. UDL benefits all kids, not just those who struggle.' www.understood.org/~

The truth is that one size does not fit all when it comes to learning and creation. We cannot create experiences for everyone; however, we can create experiences that people can access. Thinking about users and their needs whether they are in a classroom or out in the world using your digital product, there is a way to meet their needs.

Figure 1-3 shows an illustration of user-centered design (UCD).

UCD process

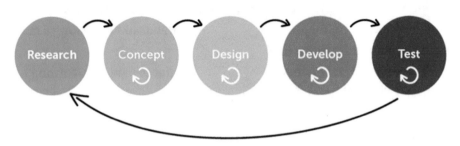

Figure 1-3. *The UCD process—research, concept, design, develop, and test.* `www.cambridgeconsultants.com/insights/untangling-ux-part-1-design-thinking-vs-ucd`

Design thinking is an iterative process in which we seek to understand the user, challenge assumptions, and redefine problems in an attempt to identify alternative strategies and solutions that might not be instantly apparent with our initial level of understanding. Figure 1-4 shows the process in an iterative way. At the same time, design thinking provides a solution-based approach to solving problems. It is a way of thinking and working as well as a collection of hands-on methods. It is not the only way of looking at problem-solving for digital experiences but by far, one of the more popular methodologies people have chosen to use. For more information, you can visit the Interaction Design Foundation web site: `www.interaction-design.org/literature/article/what-is-design-thinking-and-why-is-it-so-popular`

Design Thinking Approach

Figure 1-4. *Design thinking approach—empathize, define, ideate, prototype, and test.* `www.cambridgeconsultants.com/insights/ untangling-ux-part-1-design-thinking-vs-ucd`

In this book, I take several different approaches including universal design, design thinking, and the EVVCC (empathy, vision, values, communication and context) approach which is discussed in more detail in Chapter 5.

We Can All Create More Inclusive Experiences

We tend to think about ourselves the most, and if we are not thinking about ourselves, we are thinking about things from our organization's perspectives. It may be difficult to think about how other people may do things. We don't know if anything works until we try it out. Chapter 9 will layout testing of ideas and products and best practices.

In my classes, I incorporate Inclusive Design early on to get my students to think about creating Inclusive Product Design from the start. One of the activities I have my students do is to create an empathy map for a person who has low vision, is color blind, or is completely blind. Empathy maps are a tool to create an understanding of your users early on. It allows you to think about how your user might do the following: says, thinks, does, and feels. See the illustration in Figure 1-5.

EMPATHY MAP

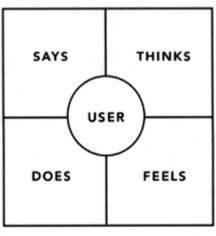

NNGROUP.COM **NN/g**

Figure 1-5. *The four quadrants of an empathy map* www.nngroup.
com/articles/empathy-mapping/

The bulleted list gives more details on what's behind the empathy map and asks questions you will need to consider and answer.

- **Empathize—Learn about your audience**: Who is my user? What matters to my audience?[3]

- **Define—Create a point of view**: What are their needs?

- **Brainstorm—Come up with creative solutions**: Wild ideas encouraged![4]

---

[3]Icons are from the 'Noun Project'
[4]Flaticon.com

- **Build a representation**: How can I show my idea? Prototype is a rough draft!

- **Share and ask for feedback**: What worked? What didn't?

True Story

In one particular class, my student sent a text message to her dad who was color blind and asked him what some of his pain points were. She received the text shown in Figure 1-6. She wrote him and said that she was working on a project in class on designing for people with color blindness. He responded with the following:

> *I don't know if this is something you're doing, but this is something you and other graphics people should know. Do not ever ever ever make charts and graphs with color coded area or bars. I cannot come close to understanding those if there are more than 3 colors. Just today I was reading an article that has a bar graph with about six or seven colors and I gave up after about two seconds. Color coded charts and graphs are just another way for The Man to keep the Brutha down. Don't use colors. Use patterns. Colors look pretty but they are completely unintelligible.*

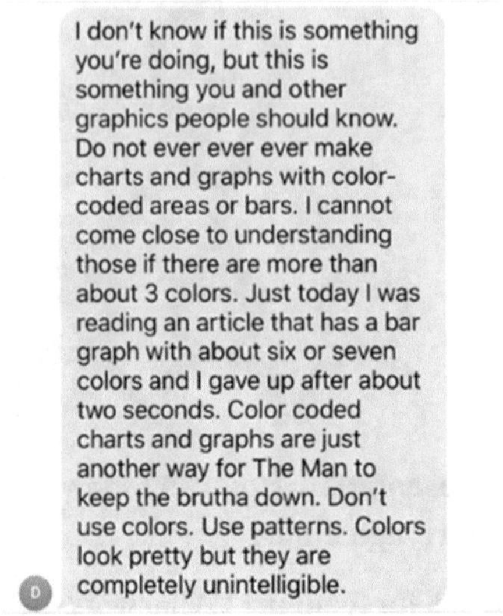

I don't know if this is something you're doing, but this is something you and other graphics people should know. Do not ever ever ever make charts and graphs with color-coded areas or bars. I cannot come close to understanding those if there are more than about 3 colors. Just today I was reading an article that has a bar graph with about six or seven colors and I gave up after about two seconds. Color coded charts and graphs are just another way for The Man to keep the brutha down. Don't use colors. Use patterns. Colors look pretty but they are completely unintelligible.

Figure 1-6. *Text message from a daughter to a father who has color blindness*

We will address how to handle color contrast in Chapter 3.

NFL Image Color Rush Uniforms

Sports are universal and many people enjoy watching or listening to sports. A great example of accessibility occurred a few years ago during the 2015 NFL season. The NFL decided that they would try using all one color for teams to wear in what they called "Color Rush" in order to celebrate the first NFL game in color 50 years prior. Figure 1-7 shows the Buffalo Bills' and New York Jets' yellow and green jerseys.

Figure 1-7. *On the left, the Buffalo Bills wearing red jerseys with blue and white stripes on the shoulders and on the side of the pants. On the right are the New York Jets wearing green jerseys with black and white strips on the shoulders and the side of the pants*

There was a problem that occurred for some people while watching the game: they could not tell which team was their team due to the colors the teams were wearing. One team was wearing red and green. For people with red–green color blindness, they were unable to see which team was their team.

What are the different types of color blindness?

The most common types of color blindness are inherited. They are the result of defects in the genes that contain the instructions for making the photopigments found in cones. Some defects alter the photopigment's sensitivity to color; for example, it might be slightly more sensitive to deeper red and less sensitive to green. Other defects can result in the total loss of a photopigment. Depending on the type of defect and the cone that is affected, problems can arise with red, green, or blue color vision.

Red–Green Color Blindness

The most common types of hereditary color blindness are due to the loss or limited function of red cone (known as protan) or green cone (deutran) photopigments. This kind of color blindness is commonly referred to as red–green color blindness.

- Protanomaly: In males with protanomaly, the red cone photopigment is abnormal. Red, orange, and yellow appear greener and colors are not as bright. This condition is mild and doesn't usually interfere with daily living. Protanomaly is an X-linked disorder estimated to affect 1% of males.

- Protanopia: In males with protanopia, there are no working red cone cells. Red appears as black. Certain shades of orange, yellow, and green all appear as yellow. Protanopia is an X-linked disorder that is estimated to affect 1 percent of males.

- Deuteranomaly: In males with deuteranomaly, the green cone photopigment is abnormal. Yellow and green appear redder, and it is difficult to tell violet from blue. This condition is mild and doesn't interfere with daily living. Deuteranomaly is the most common form of color blindness and is an X-linked disorder affecting 5% of males.

- Deuteranopia: In males with deuteranopia, there are no working green cone cells. They tend to see reds as brownish-yellow and greens as beige. Deuteranopia is an X-linked disorder that affects about 1% of males.

Blue–Yellow Color Blindness

Blue–yellow color blindness is rarer than red–green color blindness. Blue-cone (tritan) photopigments are either missing or have limited function.

- Tritanomaly: People with tritanomaly have functionally limited blue cone cells. Blue appears greener, and it can be difficult to tell yellow and red from pink. Tritanomaly is extremely rare. It is an autosomal dominant disorder affecting males and females equally.

- Tritanopia: People with tritanopia, also known as blue–yellow color blindness, lack blue cone cells. Blue appears green and yellow appears violet or light grey. Tritanopia is an extremely rare autosomal recessive disorder affecting males and females equally.

Complete Color Blindness

People with complete color blindness (monochromacy) don't experience color at all, and the clearness of their vision (visual acuity) may also be affected.

There are two types of monochromacy:

- Cone monochromacy: This rare form of color blindness results from a failure of two of the three cone cell photopigments to work. There is red cone monochromacy, green cone monochromacy, and blue cone monochromacy. People with cone monochromacy have trouble distinguishing colors because the brain needs to compare the signals from different types of cones in order to see color. When only one type of cone works, this comparison isn't possible. People with blue cone monochromacy may also have reduced visual acuity, nearsightedness, and uncontrollable eye movements, a condition known as nystagmus. Cone monochromacy is an autosomal recessive disorder.

- Rod monochromacy or achromatopsia: This type of monochromacy is rare and is the most severe form of color blindness. It is present at birth. None of the cone cells have functional photopigments. Lacking all cone vision, people with rod monochromacy see the world in black, white, and gray. And since rods respond to dim light, people with rod monochromacy tend to be photophobic—very uncomfortable in bright environments. They also experience nystagmus. Rod monochromacy is an autosomal recessive disorder.[5]

When a person has color blindness, they are not able to distinguish between certain colors. The colors look the same to them. Figure 1-8 shows real tweets addressing this issue.

---

[5]National Eye Institute "Facts about Colorblindness" https://nei.nih.gov/health/color_blindness/facts_about

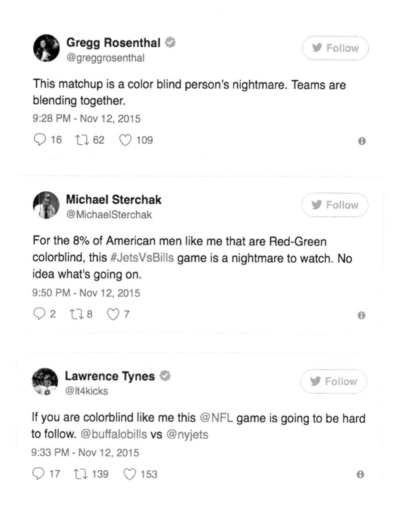

Figure 1-8. *Tweets from viewers of the NFL game between the Buffalo Bills and New York Jets*

Figure 1-9 shows how the game looked like for those with red/green color blindness (also known as deuteranomaly).

Figure 1-9. *A and B. Image A shows through a simulator what the game looked like for people with color blindness. Image B shows "Color Rush" uniforms in colors including white*

According to CBS.com, the NFL admitted that when the league was putting the "Color Rush" uniforms through the testing phases, it forgot to account for color-blind fans. After consulting with experts, the NFL changed the colors of the uniforms and added the color white because people with color blindness can distinguish white from other colors.

These examples provided go to show that user experiences are everywhere. User experience tends to be platform agnostic, and it requires us to look beyond our screens and see the world in ways which we can improve things for our users.

Many of us use the web to find what we are looking for, whether it be the latest news or a new outfit. The web is a good place for us to start to look at accessibility and to consider how some may use the web.

Where to Begin?

One of the first things I like to do when I go to a web site is to check and see if I can keyboard through the web site on my laptop or desktop. Meaning, could I actually maneuver through this web site without using a mouse? Have you ever tried it? You should!

You might ask yourself, who doesn't use a mouse? There are plenty of people who solely use a keyboard to get around the web: People who don't have the dexterity to use a mouse, people who like to only use keyboards because they find it faster to use a keyboard, and people who are visually impaired.

Where do we go from here and what can we create? In Chapter 10, we will take a look at some past innovations and future opportunities. The future is created by what you do today. Let's take a look at using the web with only your keyboard.

TRY IT YOURSELF

Go to a web site and try to only use your keyboard. See if you can tab through and notice which elements are highlighted as you go through the site.
Can you see where you should focus? Are things highlighted? Are you lost?

What may be difficult could be impossible for someone with disabilities if the access is not done properly for the device or the tools someone may use.

Conclusion

In this chapter, we covered the definitions that will be used throughout the book for accessibility and inclusivity. As a reminder, accessibility means approachability and inclusive design means making products for everyone.

One way to approach the creation of digital products is to use the W5H approach: who, what, where, when, why, and how you might approach the product. The use of design thinking or user-centered design are approaches that put the user first when creating a product.

In the next chapter, we will look at some practices related to web development in relation to headings, contrast, and navigation.

CHAPTER 2

Accessibility, Content, HTML, JavaScript, CSS, and the Land of Accessible Rich Internet Applications

Our focus in this chapter is accessibility in relation to the web. We'll cover some best practices for web development and provide sample code for you to follow along with cognitive ability.

Thus, **the impact of disability is radically changed on the Web because the Web removes barriers** to communication and interaction that many people face in the physical world. However, when web sites, applications, technologies, or tools are badly designed, they can create barriers that exclude people from using the Web.[1]

---

[1]Accessibility W3C. www.w3.org/standards/webdesign/accessibility

© Regine M. Gilbert 2019
R. M. Gilbert, *Inclusive Design for a Digital World*,
https://doi.org/10.1007/978-1-4842-5016-7_2

"Accessibility is essential for developers and organizations that want to create high quality websites and web tools, and not exclude people from using their products and services." W3C

Key concepts covered include

- Web standards defined

- Importance of web content

- HTML (H1, H2, H3, and SEO)

- CSS (color contrast)

- JavaScript (navigation)

- ARIA (Accessible Rich Internet Applications)

Governing on the Web

In Figure 2-1, there is a set of stairs and ramps with handrails. Take a look, and using the W5H (who, what, where, when, why, how) approach, ask yourself the following questions:

- Who can use this entrance/exit?

- What do you see when you look at this photo?

- When will people enter or exit?

- Why would people use the ramp or stairs?

- How does this apply to the digital world?

Figure 2-1. *Photo of stairs with a ramp. Handrails are only on the stairs*

Taking a closer look at the ramp and stairs, notice the steepness of the ramp, notice there are no rails where the ramps are and that there are only rails for two out of four sets of the stairs.

Is this really accessible? No, it is not. In many instances, what we think is accessible is often times not and that depends on many factors including the design. This is an easy way to think about web accessibility—or really, how you might not have been thinking about web accessibility. Similar to the ramp in Figure 2-1, you might think because there's a ramp, it's accessible to everyone. But in this case, it can definitely be more accessible-friendly, and there's room for us to question what can be improved upon.

One of the things that can help us understand what to do are regulating legislation like the American with Disabilities Act[2] for structures and the web. The web has a governing body called the World Wide Web Consortium (W3C).

W3C is the entity that developed web standards for users of the web around the globe. The W3C is made up of people from all over the world and, at the time of this publication, is headed up by Tim Berners Lee (the inventor of the web) and CEO Jeffrey Jaffe. W3C developed standards when it comes to making the web accessible, calling it the "Web Content Accessibility Guidelines" (WCAG). In 2018, 10 years after the creation of WCAG 2.0, a new version has emerged to incorporate mobile accessibility standards, among many other changes.

> *The power of the Web is in its universality. Access by everyone regardless of disability is an essential aspect.*
>
> —Tim Berners-Lee

Web Accessibility

W3C defines "web accessibility" as websites, tools, and technologies designed and developed so that people with disabilities can use them.[3] More specifically through web accessibility, people can

- Perceive, understand, navigate, and interact with the web

- Contribute to the web

---

[2]The Americans with Disabilities Act (ADA) became a law in 1990. The ADA is a civil rights law that prohibits discrimination against individuals with disabilities in all areas of public life, including jobs, schools, transportation, and all public and private places that are open to the general public. *National Network. "What is the ADA"* https://adata.org/learn-about-ada (accessed on January 31, 2019)

[3]W3C. *"Fundamentals of Accessibility".* www.w3.org/WAI/fundamentals/accessibility-intro/#context (accessed December 5, 2018)

Web accessibility encompasses all disabilities, including

- Auditory

- Cognitive

- Neurological

- Physical

- Speech

- Visual

Web accessibility also benefits people without disabilities, for example

- People using mobile phones, smart watches, smart TVs, and other devices with small screens, different input modes, etc.

- Older people with changing abilities due to aging

- People with "temporary disabilities" such as a broken arm or lost glasses

- People with "situational limitations" such as in bright sunlight or in an environment where they cannot listen to audio

- People using a slow Internet connection or who have limited or expensive bandwidth

Many of us are using the Internet and other digital products every single day. Approximately 3 billion people are on the Internet right now! Digital products are all around us, and in order to best serve those who use them, we need to ensure accessibility.

Web Content

More than half of the world's population is on the Internet. What might they be looking at? Regardless of the details of that answer, they are looking at content, and that content is the main reason any of visit any web site.

A proper layout of content is important for any readership. Typically, content is provided by content strategists and copywriters, but this varies by organization. When first organizing a product, it's good to start with knowing what type of content you will provide. Content, page layout and hierarchy are important for readability. We will dive deeper into accessible web content in Chapter 5.

When it comes to accessibility and content, there are some key layout "best practices" to follow. For a more inclusive experience, overall, content should be placed in a way that is understandable.

Titles, headings, and links should be clearly visible upon first glance since this is the way that many people scan a site. This is also the way assistive technologies, such as screen readers (typically used by people with visual impairments), read a page.

When looking at a web page, you can break out the content of a page into the following categories:

- Headers

- Titles

- Paragraphs

- Images

- Forms

- Links

On each page of a product application, the title should be unique and the hierarchy of the page should reflect the content. We want to clearly indicate and manage focus. To do so, you should always ask,

"What is most important?" In Figure 2-2 we can see headers, and the importance of those headers is clearly shown by the font size.

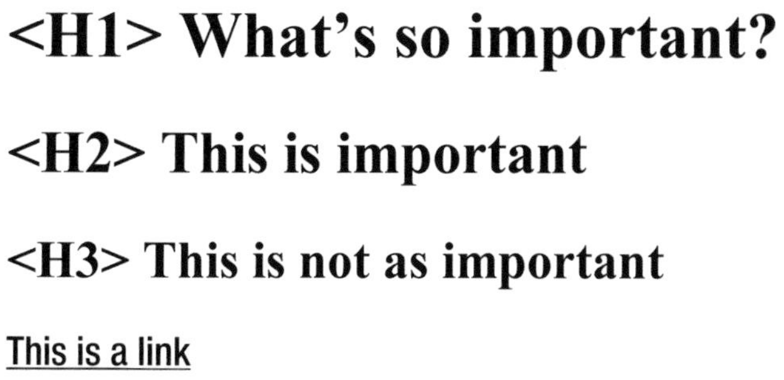

\<H1\> What's so important?

\<H2\> This is important

\<H3\> This is not as important

This is a link

Figure 2-2. *Content hierarchy. Each header has a level of importance based on the size and location on the page*

Headers should be reflective of the most important things on the page. Paragraphs will contain text in sentence form and links should clearly reflect where the user is going to go next and should have enough contrast.

When organizing the content, you need to ensure that you use proper hierarchy and associate the proper headings. Information architecture and content strategy play an important role in the design of digital products.

Information Architecture Helps Build Better Experiences

Information Architects (IA) organize digital products. When you think of the massive amounts of data out there, it all needs to be structured in some way, and this is what an IA can do.

A prominent information architect is Abby the IA. Abby is an independent information architecture, and one of the approaches she takes to information is to look at the why, what, and how (Figure 2-3).

Abby has the following definitions for the Why, What, and How:

- Why: Reasons

- What: Specification

- How: Execution

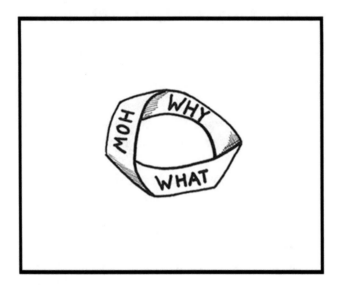

Define Why, What & How

Figure 2-3.   *The loop of How, Why, What, and How from Abby the IA*[4]

Information architecture helps designers, developers, and content
strategists do their jobs better when they can specify the reasons, the
specifications associated with what needs to be done, and how to execute
those specifications.

What type of content might your product include? Will there be
images, text, and forms? How will you organize this information? More
times than not, the content of your product is not available before

---

[4]Abby the IA. "Define why, what & how" http://abbytheia.com/2014/06/30/
define-why-what-how/ Accessed on January 31, 2019

development. However, it is best practice to develop the content ahead
of the design by introducing a content model. In Carrie Hanes and Mike
Atherton's book *Designing Connected Content,* they recommend starting
with a content-first strategy. This will give structure for the creation of
different representations and interfaces (think about how your users may
access your product via mobile, desktop, or a voice application), allowing
people to efficiently navigate through the content.

Figure 2-4 is an example of a simplified content model I've used in
practice. You will want to think of your audience, the purpose of the page,
and questions they may ask.

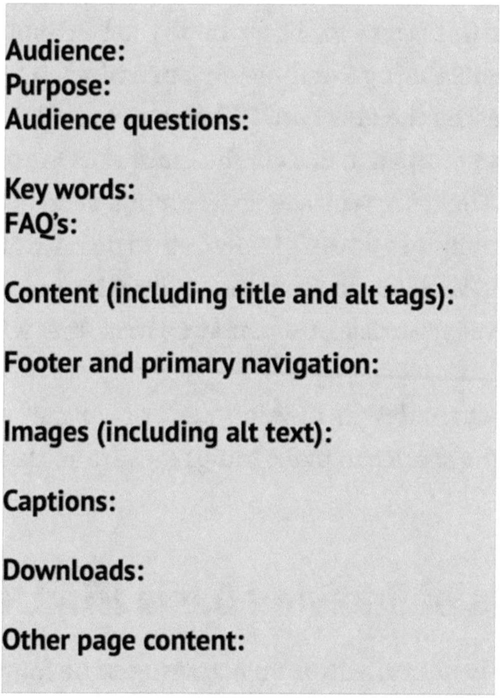

Audience:
Purpose:
Audience questions:

Key words:
FAQ's:

Content (including title and alt tags):

Footer and primary navigation:

Images (including alt text):

Captions:

Downloads:

Other page content:

Figure 2-4. *Example of content model: audience, purpose, audience
questions, keywords, FAQ's, content (including title and alt tags),
footer and primary navigation, images, captions, downloads, and
other page content*

After development of the content, your product will then be ready
to be built. There are many ways to build web pages these days, and for
the purposes of this book, we will focus on HTML, CSS, JavaScript, and
ARIA. Development of a product takes a team effort and so does creating
accessible products. Now we'll go into more detail about each of those steps.

What Does the Code Do?

Whether you are building things yourself or working closely with those who
build digital products, it is helpful to understand how things work. If you
are already familiar with building products, this may be a refresher for you
and for those who this is new to, it's my hope you learn something new.

While on a panel during Computer Science Week in November of 2018,
a young student asked the question, "What does code do?" The three of us
on the panel were stumped to answer the question. One of the panelists
then answered, "The things you see on a computer screen have to be
programmed. A computer doesn't know how to do anything unless you
tell it how to do it." With this in mind, not only will people be reading the
content of whatever you create, there may be machines who read what you
create as well

Whether you are in design, development, or any part of the creative
process, you get the chance to make things that are accessible to those who
may access it.

The Benefits of Knowing Basic HTML and CSS

Designers would benefit greatly from acquiring some foundational
knowledge of what's called the "front end" (the presentation layer) driven
by HTML (Hyper Text Markup Language) and CSS (Cascading Style Sheets,
a language that describes the component styles in an HTML document)
and would perhaps be surprised by how easy it is to learn the basics.

HTML and CSS don't involve programming logic. The letter M in HTML stands for "Markup," a way to describe the coded structure of page elements which are the building blocks of pages. HTML with CSS and JavaScript form a triad of foundational technologies for the World Wide Web.

In layman's terms, HTML is an architectural map that tells the browser **what** to display, and CSS, or Cascading Style Sheets, is the code that tells the browser how to display things.

Metaphorically speaking, if HTML is the skeleton of a page, CSS would describe the height, the body shape, the skin, eye color, hair color, etc. The language has a very simple code structure that determines typography, colors, positions, and dimensions.

Understanding Code and How to Code Is Understanding Pixels

Learning how to code the front-end UI and previewing it gives designers the opportunity to immediately see how things are displayed when viewed on various devices. If designers play with HTML and CSS, they'll notice that everything is measured in pixels (there are other measurement units such as "ems" and percentages that will ultimately be converted to pixels).

Understanding measurements and code structure, that is, how pages are displayed, will provide a deeper understanding of the front-end development process. That in turn will cause designers think more deeply about their designs and how to make them more efficient for that process. They will know what can be easily achieved and what would be more challenging.[5]

Alongside an understanding of code, it is also helpful to understand assistive technologies that people with disabilities may use in order to access the code.

---

[5]Coding for designers: How much should we know www.toptal.com/designers/
ui-ux-designers/designers-coding

Assistive Technologies

Screen readers is a software technology, typically used by people who are visually impaired, that reads the content of a web page or application. Someone using a screen reader can then use a keyboard to "see" a web site.

The American Federation for the Blind (AFB) defines screen readers as software programs that allow blind or visually impaired users to read the text that is displayed on the computer screen with a speech synthesizer or braille display.[6] A screen reader is the interface between the computer's operating system, its applications, and the user.

Let's go into more detail about how it works:

- The user sends commands by pressing different combinations of keys on the computer keyboard or braille display to instruct the speech synthesizer on what to say and to speak automatically when changes occur on the computer screen.

- A command can instruct the synthesizer to read or spell a word, read a line or full screen of text, find a string of text on the screen, announce the location of the computer's cursor or focused item, and so on.

- In addition, it allows users to perform more advanced functions, such as locating text displayed in a certain color, reading predesignated parts of the screen on demand, reading highlighted text, and identifying the active choice on a menu.

- Users may also use the spell checker in a word processor or read the cells of a spreadsheet with a screen reader.

---

[6]The American Federation for the Blind. "*Screen Readers*". www.afb.org/ prodBrowseCatResults.aspx?CatID=49 (accessed December 5, 2018)

Screen readers are built into many Macs and PCs and there is also additional software that can be purchased. Three of the most popular are

- JAWS

- NVDA

- VoiceOver

For our purposes, in this book, we'll focus on the areas of headings, keyboard navigation, forms, images, languages, and tab functionality.

It is of key importance that web pages have a H1 which should match the title of the page as shown in Figure 2-2. If you are looking for a resource on coding inclusive experiences, I highly recommend Heydon Pickering's book *Inclusive Design Patterns*.

HTML Best Practices

Let's revisit what could be included in the content of a page:

- Headers

- Titles

- Paragraphs

- Images

- Forms

- Links

We can apply HTML (Hyper Text Markup Language) to the content: headers, titles, paragraphs, images, forms, and links. Adding styling to a web page could include CSS and JavaScript which we will talk about a little later.

There are many resources for developers such as Mozilla's resources for developers by developers (Figure 2-5).

Figure 2-5. *Resources for developers by developers.* `https://`
`developer.mozilla.org/en-US/`

Knowledge of semantic HTML can improve the accessibility of web sites. Think of a house without a frame; that's what a web site might be without semantic HTML. Assistive technologies, such as screen readers, will read HTML and then users can control the degree of details that the screen reader engages and shares with the user.

Use Container Elements for Layout Only

Elements like `<div>` and `<span>` are for layout only. They're semantically meaningless, they don't have keyboard or touch support in any browser, and they don't communicate anything to the accessibility API. For example, never use a `div` or `span` for a button when you could use a semantically meaningful button element.

Use Other HTML Elements the Way They're Intended

All of the other HTML elements should be used to tell the browser what functional purpose your content serves. The other HTML elements provide meaning to the browser and assistive technology about what you're saying

on your web site. You should choose them based on what the content is—
not based on how they look with graphics.

Use the following HTML elements to structure every page:

- header

- nav

- main

- article

- aside

- footer

Headings

- Use one H1 per page and have it match the page title.

- Do not skip heading levels when increasing, but you
  can skip levels when decreasing (h1, h2, h3, h2, h3, h4,
  h2, h3, h4).

- The headings taken out of context should logically
  represent the page content for screen readers and users
  who choose this option as a way to scan the page.[7]

Examples of Accessibility Do's and Don'ts for HTML

In Figures 2-6 through 2-8, we see examples of how to set up a page using
HTML elements. In Figure 2-6 we see an example of a "title" page and the
correct way to do it.

---

[7]http://web-accessibility.carnegiemuseums.org/foundations/semantic/

```
<!-- Example 1 -->
<!-- Always Include a Page Title in the Head -->
<!-- Do This -->

  <head>
    <meta charset="utf-8">
    <title> Special Pizza NYC </title>
  </head>
  <body>
```

Figure 2-6. *Always include a title in the <head> section of a page.
This helps screen readers as well as web crawlers for search engine
optimization*

```
<!-- Example 2 -->
<!-- Be as explicit as possible when using tags and always include headings for main titles --
<!-- Do This -->

<h1>Special Pizza NYC</h1>
  <h2>About Special Pizza</h2>
    <h3>Our Story</h3>
    <h3>Our Founder</h3>
  <h2>Why Our Pizza Is Special</h2>
    <h3>Our Ingredients</h3>
    <h3>Our Chef</h3>

<!-- Not This -->
<div>Special Pizza NYC</div>
<div>About Special Pizza</div>
<div>Why Our Pizza is Special</div>
```

Figure 2-7. *Be as explicit as possible when using tags and always
include headings for main titles; see Figure 2-7 for an example*

```
<!-- Example 3 -->
<!-- Add alternate text descriptions to images -->
<!-- Do This -->

<img src="http://pizza.photos.jpg" alt="photo of pepperoni pizza">

<!-- Not This -->

<img src="http://pizza.photos.jpg">
```

Figure 2-8. *Here's an example of using* alt *to add a text description to images. Alt text is a phrase that can take the place of an image for screen readers or if an image isn't rendering properly*

As we can see, semantic HTML is important for the structure of pages and it helps the hierarchy of the page in a way that is not only accessible but more readable for all of us.

HTML provides initials structure and CSS (Cascading Style Sheets) provides the style of the page in relation to the layout and colors. In this section, we will address color contrast, hiding content, and order. Table 2-1 shows WCAG 2.1 Color Guidelines.

Table 2-1. *WCAG 2.1 Color Guidelines*

Success Criterion 1.4.1 Use of Color	(Level A)	Color is not used as the only visual means of conveying information, indicating an action, prompting a response, or distinguishing a visual element
Success Criterion 1.4.3 Contrast (Minimum)	(Level AA)	The visual presentation of text and images of text has a contrast ratio of at least 4.5:1
Success Criterion 1.4.6 Contrast (Enhanced)	(Level AAA)	The visual presentation of text and images of text has a contrast ratio of at least 7:1

WCAG 2.1 states that color is not used as the only visual means of
conveying information, indicating an action, prompting a response, or a
distinguishing element.[8]

For example, let's review Figure 2-9. There are two rectangles with grey
backgrounds. One illustrates the use of accessible ratio, which is easier to
read and the other illustrates an inaccessible ratio, which is a little harder
to read. It is important to use the proper colors to separate the foreground
and background.

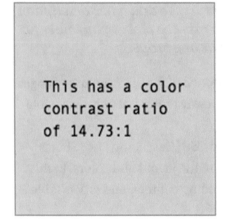
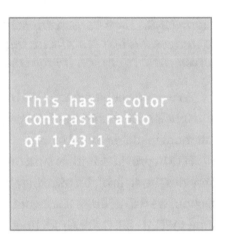

Figure 2-9. *Color contrast ratios according to WCAG 2.1. The left
image is accessible, while the right image is not*

Luckily you don't have to be an expert when it comes to color contrast
ratios. You can measure color contrast using a color contrast checker
through various web sites or plugins. A list is provided in the Appendix.

The best way to learn is by doing, so let's check out the HTML and CSS
of one of your favorite web sites. In the following, we provide you with the
steps to check out the inspector tools using Chrome, Firefox, or Safari.

---

[8]https://www.w3.org/TR/WCAG21/#use-of-color

TRY IT YOURSELF

Check out the HTML and CSS of a website:

<u>Chrome</u>

1. Right-click an element or a blank area on the web page. Select "Inspect" from the popup menu.

2. Use the Chrome menu to access the More Tools ➤ Developer tools option.[9]

<u>Firefox</u>

1. Right-click an element or a blank area on the web page. Select "Inspect Element" from the popup menu.

2. From the Firefox menu, click Web Developer ➤ Inspector.[10]

<u>Safari</u>

1. Right-click or control-click an element or blank area on the web page.

2. Click Develop in the menu bar and select Open Web Inspector in the popup menu that appears. If you don't see Develop in the menu bar, pull down the Safari menu and choose Preferences,

---

[9]Tools for developers. *"Inspect and Edit Pages and Styles"* `https://developers.google.com/web/tools/chrome-devtools/inspect-styles/` (Accessed on November 29, 2018)

[10]Firefox Developer Tools. *"Firefox Developer Tools"* `https://developer.mozilla.org/en-US/docs/Tools` (Accessed on November 29, 2018)

click the Advanced tab, and check the box next to show

Develop menu in menu bar.

3. Click individual elements of the web page to see the code
   devoted to that particular section.[11]

JavaScript

JavaScript, a language used with HTML and CSS, provides interactivity on web sites, an important aspect when we are talking about accessibility. In this section, we'll focus on navigation and user control with JavaScript.

Being able to keyboard through a site is a key factor of accessibility. Buttons, modals, and focus can be controlled through JavaScript. For accessibility purposes, it is best to limit the amount of JavaScript used. It's best to focus on semantic HTML and CSS.

> *When it comes to using Javascript, less is more. You can get a lot of similar effects with CSS.*
>
> —Donovan Taitt
> Full Stack Developer and
> Software Engineering Instructor
> at General Assembly

Making an accessible site doesn't mean that you have to decide whether to use JavaScript or not. Accessibility is about making content available to as many people as possible, which also includes users with old browsers and computers, slow Internet connections, strict security restrictions (e.g., no JavaScript), and so on. The experience under conditions like these where JavaScript may not

---

[11]Safari User Guide. "Developer Tools" https://support.apple.com/guide/safari/use-the-developer-tools-in-the-develop-menu-sfri20948/mac (Accessed on November 29, 2018)

work or take too long to load might not be ideal but is still good enough if the web site is accessible and usable.[12]

There is a time and place for everything, and JavaScript can be used with Accessible Rich Internet Applications (ARIA). ARIA is good for bridging areas with accessibility issues that can't be managed with native HTML. It works by allowing you to specify attributes that modify the way an element is translated into the accessibility tree. Let's look at an example.

In the following code snippet, we use a list item as a kind of custom checkbox. The CSS "checkbox" class gives the element the required visual characteristics.

```
<li tabindex="0" class="checkbox" checked>
  Receive promotional offers
</li>
```

While this works fine for sighted users, a screen reader will give no indication that the element is meant to be a checkbox, so low-vision users may miss the element entirely.

Using ARIA attributes, however, we can give the element the missing information so the screen reader can properly interpret it. Here, we've added the role and ARIA-checked attributes to explicitly identify the element as a checkbox and specify that it is checked by default. The list item will now be added to the accessibility tree and a screen reader will correctly report it as a checkbox.[13]

```
<li tabindex="0" class="checkbox" role="checkbox" checked
aria-checked="true">
  Receive promotional offers
</li>
```

---

[12]Manual Matuzovic Writing JavaScript with accessibility in mind https://medium. com/@matuzo/writing-javascript-with-accessibility-in-mind-a1f6a5f467b9

[13]https://developers.google.com/web/fundamentals/accessibility/ semantics-aria/

Conclusion

Content plays an important role in regard to what your users may or may not be able to access. Information architecture and layout of pages has an impact on accessibility and can disrupt the use of your product if not done in a proper way.

Using a combination of HTML, CSS, JavaScript, and ARIA can create a better experience from an accessibility standpoint. Here are a few things to consider to keep you on track:

- Clearly indicate and manage focus.

- Ensure users can visually track their focus when keyboard navigating.

- Keep users focused on controls.

- Semantic HTML—Make the content accessible (accessible content tips in Chapter 5).

- Use Action words as links—put periods for abbreviations (e.g., F.B.I).

- Present links in an obvious and consistent way.

- Include images used as icons or bullets in the link.

- Use simple, clear navigation cues and labels.

CHAPTER 3

If It's Annoying, It's Probably not Accessible

One of the best things in life is the ability to never stop learning.

Learning more and more about accessibility has brought about the knowledge that if something is annoying, it's probably not accessible. An annoyance is something that causes some irritation in some sort of way. Picture this scenario.

Imagine being at a conference and sitting in a room that housed 1100 chairs (Figure 3-1 shows the back of the conference room). You are a little late to the start of the presentation and you decide to sit in the very back of the room.

There are two large screens at the front of the room. The presenter is on the stage, begins speaking, and starts their slide show. As they are talking, you look at the slides only to realize that you cannot see anything on the slides at all. Although you can pay attention to what the person is saying, you cannot make out much of anything. So you take out your phone to take a photo of the screen so you can zoom in to see what they are talking about, and when you do that, you look at the photo, only to see it's just as blurry as what you see in front of you.

© Regine M. Gilbert 2019
R. M. Gilbert, *Inclusive Design for a Digital World*,
https://doi.org/10.1007/978-1-4842-5016-7_3

Figure 3-1. *Conference room at HOW Design Live 2018*

This is an example of an annoying experience from an audience perspective. It is the responsibility of the conference and the presenter to ensure that the information on the screen is as clear for the person in the front of the room as it is for the person in the back of the room.

Unfortunately, this happened to me when I did a presentation at HOW Design Live in 2018 speaking about accessibility. It is what prompted me to write this chapter. Although I read everything that was on the slides during my presentation, and the conference provided sign language interpreters, the typeface on my slides were too small, and in the end, my accessibility talk was not accessible to many people who were sitting further than five rows back.

In this chapter, we will cover annoying things in relation to digital products and how often things that are annoying are probably not accessible. It's important to note that often things that are annoying are inaccessible and therefore exclude people with disabilities.

The Annoyances and Solutions

In the following sections, we will cover these areas and list best practices to correct them:

- Pages take too long to load
- Poor functionality of desktop site
- App leads to web site
- Links going to different places/dead links
- Poor content layout
- Pop-ups
- Icons not clear
- FONTS ALL CAPS
- Too much text
- Text spans the full width
- Misplaced button boxes
- AutoPlay

This list came from asking many of my past students, family members, and anyone I had the chance to ask, "What do you find annoying about web site/apps/digital products?" As we walk through these annoyances, we will note possible solution and the Web Content Accessibility Guidelines (WCAG) that would make it not so annoying and accessible. It's good to remember that user experience starts at the moment the project begins. Using W5H (who, what, where, when, why, and how) as creators, we can think about what we are building in relation to our users.

A Page Taking Too Long to Load

When you go on a site and you are waiting to see the page and nothing happens. As you sit there and wait for it to appear, you might see some sort of indicator that the page is loading. When someone is using assistive technologies, they are waiting without seeing the wait indicator. We are in the 21st century and there is an expectation that when we visit a page, we will be able to view it right away. There are several reasons for pages taking a long time to load due to image size or errors.

There is an option in HTML to alert screen reader users the way that sighted users are notified with an indicator.

The following code snippet shows how the alert role is added directly into the html source code.

```
<h2 role="alert">Your form could not be submitted because of 3
validation errors.</h2>
```

The moment the element finishes loading, the screen reader should be alerted. If the element was already in the original source code when the page loaded, the screen reader will announce the error immediately after announcing the page title. You always want to orient the user as to where they are and what they are doing. Any alert or indicator is good for them to experience.

Poor Content Layout

Poor content layout is often times due to out-of-place hierarchy. In Chapter 2, we discussed the importance of hierarchy when it comes to layout and accessibility. Proper hierarchy allows your users to scan the page in a logical way. In Figure 3-2, we see a page of imagery with large text. The focus is on the larger text and the real message is with the smaller text. Figure 3-2 reads "Poor Content Layout" as the larger text and "Pay attention to hierarchy" as the smaller text.

Figure 3-2. *Example of large text imagery*

Content layout is in relation to the WCAG 2.1 success criterion 1.3.1, 1.3.2, and 1.3.3.[1] Here are the standards:

- Success Criterion 1.3.1 Info and Relationships (Level A): Information, structure, and relationships conveyed through presentation can be programmatically determined or are available in text.

- Success Criterion 1.3.2 Meaningful Sequence (Level A): When the sequence in which content is presented affects its meaning, a correct reading sequence can be programmatically determined.

---

[1] www.w3.org/TR/WCAG21/

- Success Criterion 1.3.3 Sensory Characteristics
  (Level A): Instructions provided for understanding
  and operating content do not rely solely on sensory
  characteristics of components such as shape, color,
  size, visual location, orientation, or sound.

We want to provide users with an opportunity to explore our content but in the way in which is guided by the design. Set up what is next for users in a way that aligns with their expectations.

Pop-ups

Beloved pop-ups! I have designed many pop-up (otherwise known as modals) during my time as a designer. A lot of businesses feel they are good for the collection of emails and the numbers don't lie! People engage with them. Out of everyone I asked, no one likes pop-ups and yet we still use them.

The annoyance with pop-ups is that they interrupt whatever we were about to do. When asked about the biggest pain point people experience, "not being able to close the pop-up" was a high on their list.

There are options to improve this experience overall. One way is to ensure that you are providing the right affordances to allow the user to close the pop-up once it appears. Another way is to use proper color contrast so users can distinguish between the background and the foreground.

When it comes to code, there are several options as well. One of them is to manage focus for the user. To restrict focus to just the modal dialog, you will need to use JavaScript to put focus on the dialog container (i.e., the `<article>` element) and then force focus back onto the dialog if the focus leaves.

The article "Making an accessible dialog box" by Nicholas C. Zakas (`https://handbook.floeproject.org/ModalDialogs.html`) outlines the JavaScript required to manage the dialog interaction correctly. See Listing 3-1 for an example.

Listing 3-1. Modal Dialog Markup Example

```
<article role="dialog" aria-labelledby="dialogTitle" aria-
describedby="dialogContents" aria-hidden="false">
    <h1 id="dialogTitle">Send email without a subject?</h1>
    <p id="dialogContents">Are you sure you want to send the
    email without a subject?</p>
    <input type="button" value="No">
    <input type="button" value="Yes">
</article>
```

Too Much Text

Too much text can be annoying because you may feel overwhelmed. For instance, when people with dyslexia[2] view too much text, they may not be able to distinguish between the letters. One way to alleviate too much text is referring back to hierarchy and page layout.

Ensuring that you use a proper layout that is understandable can help people move through the content. Breaking the content into different pages and not putting everything on one page is another solution.

Some additional recommendations:

- Use readable fonts for the web (i.e., sans-serif fonts).

- Build readable layouts.

- Use complete sentences.

- Use proper contrast between foreground and background.

In the end, you want the individuals using your product to complete their goals so that you, as a business, can continue to grow.

---

[2]Dyslexia is a learning disability that impairs a person's fluency or accuracy in being able to read, write, and spell.

Uncertainty Related to Buttons and Links

When it comes to buttons or links, sometimes they are understandable and sometimes they are not, and when they are not, it can be frustrating. It can also mean that a task is impossible for some to complete if they are using assistive technology and things are not clear. Figure 3-3 shows what a button is vs. a link. Not only is this important to sighted users to distinguish, it is also critical for assistive technologies to know the difference so that the individual can know what to do next.

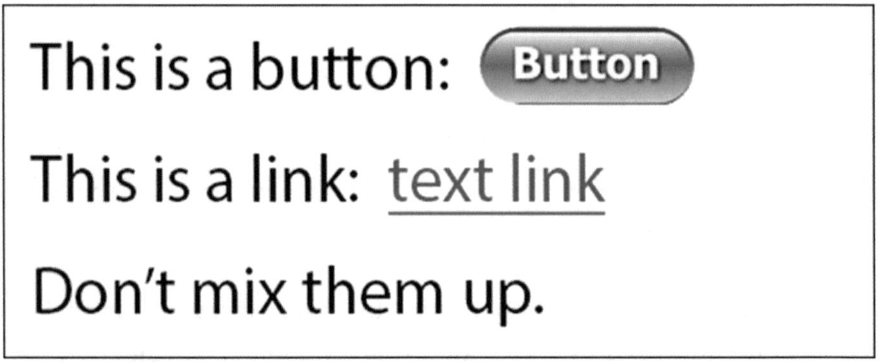

This is a button: **Button**

This is a link: <u>text link</u>

Don't mix them up.

Figure 3-3. *(Source: Web Axe* `www.webaxe.org/proper-use-buttons-links/`*)*

As creators, our goal is to release products that allow the individual to control their experience. By not properly naming assets, like buttons or links, we take away control from the users and, in the process, increase friction between the individual and the product. WCAG SC 1.3.5, 1.3.6, and 2.2.6 cover a lot of this. Here is the summary of these from Level Access.[3]

- SC 1.3.5 Identify Input Purpose (AA): For content created with markup languages, the purpose of specific input fields indicated in WCAG 2.1 needs

---

[3]`www.levelaccess.com/wcag-2-1-exploring-new-success-criteria/`

to be communicated programmatically such as via the autocomplete attribute in HTML. The purpose can then be transformed by personalization tools to communicate this in different ways such as via icons or symbols to assist users with cognitive and learning disabilities.

- SC 1.3.6 Identify Purpose (AAA): This builds on SC 1.3.5 and includes communicating purpose for icons, regions, links, buttons, and other user interface elements, to support personalization for people with cognitive and learning disabilities.

- SC 2.2.6 Timeouts (AAA): When a timeout is used, advise users of the duration of inactivity that will cause the timeout and result in loss of data. Users with cognitive disabilities or other focus/memory-related disabilities may require more time to read content or to complete interactions, such as completing an order form. The use of timed events can present barriers for people who need to take breaks. Providing the duration of inactivity before a timeout occurs will help users plan for breaks.

When there is a call to action and the individual needs to make a choice, you want to make that as clear as possible for them.

Autoplay

Autoplay can also be called making things impossible.

Saved the best for last: Autoplay is when videos play on their own without the individual having any control over the start and stop. Figure 3-4 shows some tweets of how people feel about Netflix's autoplay.

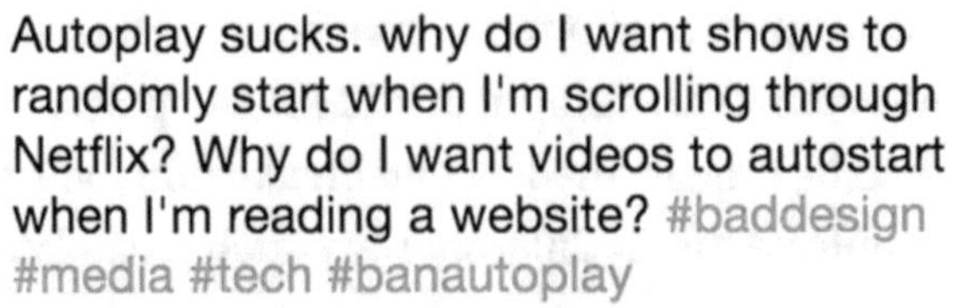

Autoplay sucks. why do I want shows to randomly start when I'm scrolling through Netflix? Why do I want videos to autostart when I'm reading a website? #baddesign #media #tech #banautoplay

Figure 3-4. *Tweets about Netflix autoplay functionality*

Not only is autoplay an issue when it comes to videos, it also happens with music. This is an issue for so many reasons including the fact that videos and flashes can trigger seizures in individuals as well as cause panic and anxiety when sound is suddenly blared loudly. Not only is autoplay annoying, it can be dangerous.

There are ways to show the content you want, while allowing the user to have control.

- Add a play/stop button to allow the user to have control

- If you must have autoplay, have the video only play once

- Refrain from using audio and opt to have captions with transcripts available

In the world of balancing business needs and user goals, it is important to remember that happy individuals will engage more with your businesses, and when they are not happy they will let you know it. As creators, we have a responsibility to the business and the individual. When we make things less annoying, we actually make them more accessible and ultimately we want individuals to have delightful experiences.

WCAG 2.1 criteria 1.4.2 Audio Control[4] states: "Success Criterion 1.4.2 Audio Control (Level A): If any audio on a Web page plays automatically for more than 3 seconds, either a mechanism is available to pause or stop the audio, or a mechanism is available to control audio volume independently from the overall system volume level."

---

[4]www.w3.org/WAI/WCAG21/Understanding/audio-control

Case Study: Manipulative (Dark) Patterns

Manipulative patterns, also known as dark patterns, are designed to manipulate us into getting users to do something that they might not have intended to do or stay on with a subscription when they really want to unsubscribe. Figure 3-5 shows unsubscribe options a user may have with an option to "unsubscribe to all"; notice how the option is not underlined so there is no indicator you could tap or click.

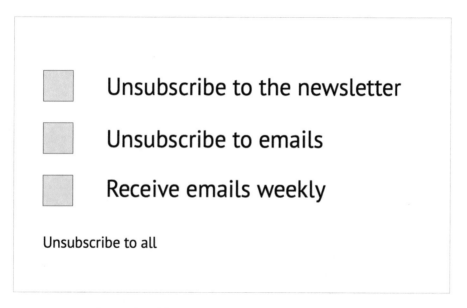

Figure 3-5. *Three checkbox options —"Unsubscribe to the newsletter," "unsubscribe to emails," "receive emails weekly," and an option to select "unsubscribe to all"*

WTF—what is the focus? We don't really know what we should choose. This example is meant to deceive the user and keep them subscribed to email and newsletters.

Case Study: From ABC Science

There is nothing better than a first-person account of a scenario. This case study from ABC science tells Dr. Scott Hollier's experience with manipulative (dark) patterns. Dr. Hollier is legally blind. The case study expresses the importance of how designs can be made for ease of use or can cause friction.

Scott Hollier logged into an online portal recently and was immediately faced with a familiar yet irritating Internet question: "How many of these pictures include buses?"

CAPTCHA security tests, or the "Completely Automated Public Turing Test to Tell Computers and Humans Apart," are not always accessible to people with disabilities—sometimes putting them, ridiculously, in the "robot" category (Figure 3-6).

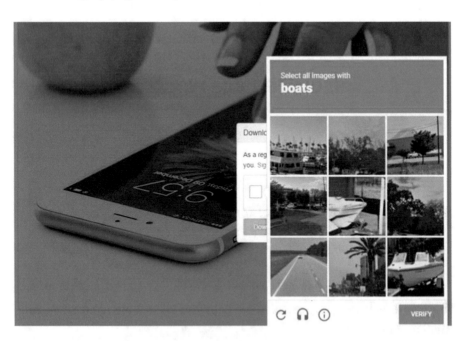

Figure 3-6. *IMAGE CAPTCHA messages, which asked Internet users to pass visual tests, can be a problem for people with a vision impairment. (Pixabay: Stevepb)*

"I had two choices," said Dr. Hollier, a digital access specialist who is legally blind.

"I could either not do what I needed to do for my work or I could ask my 11-year-old son to come figure it out for me."

These moments of friction or "encoded inhospitality," as accessibility advocate Chancey Fleet has put it, block nonvisual access to everyday digital interactions.

She also calls them "dark patterns"—a term popularized by British user-experience consultant Harry Brignull, which describes online techniques that manipulate users. A completely fake online countdown, for example.

Ms. Fleet said that while most conversations about dark patterns focus on design choices that nudge, deceive, and distract, the concept should extend to "inhospitable design features arising from inattention, neglect, and false assumptions about the capabilities and desires of disabled people."

For people who are blind or vision impaired, such roadblocks can "come and go without documentation, explanation or apology," she wrote in an email.

"Dark Patterns" Everywhere

Like asking your son to help you get past CAPTCHA, the onus is often on people who have a disability to use workarounds when they encounter "dark patterns" online.

If not, accounts are not set up, purchases are not made and full participation in the online economy and conversation is elided.

Think of navigating a football ticket purchase with a screen reader that converts text to audio or braille only to have the web page time out because you took longer than the allotted 8 minutes.

Dr. Hollier has taken on CAPTCHA in particular, writing advice for the World Wide Web Consortium that offers alternative methods for web site designers that are less exclusionary.

"The oldest CAPTCHA is the one with the squiggly letters, which are almost impossible to read under the best of circumstances," Dr. Hollier said.

"And understandably, people who are blind can't do those ones either. And the audio CAPTCHAs are terrible as well."

Web accessibility consultant Mark Muscat said webform instructions can also be problematic—interactive calendars can be needlessly difficult to navigate, for example, when picking a date for a flight or a move.

It's also just bad for business. "If people can't use a website within...30 seconds, they're going to go look somewhere else," he said.

While many online services have accessibility features, they're not always implemented by default—another dark pattern, in Ms. Fleet's view.

Figure 3-7 shows a screenshot of the Accessibility window on Twitter.

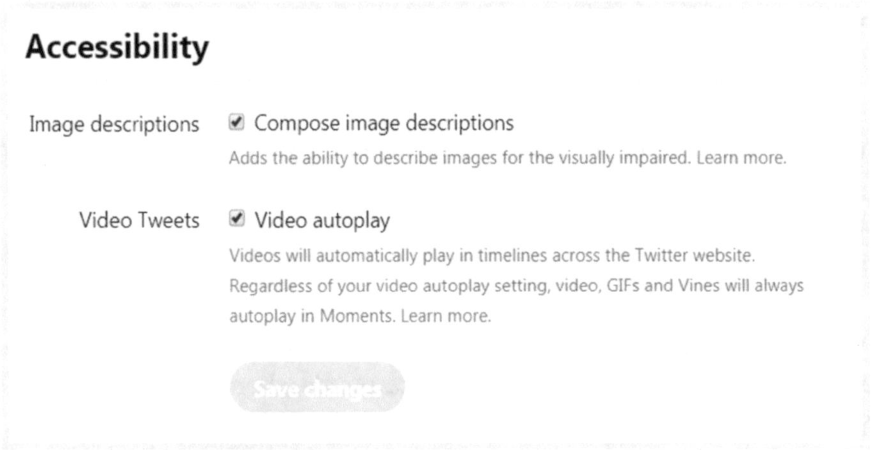

Figure 3-7. *INFOGRAPHIC on Twitter, the ability to add image descriptions are not on by default. (ABC News: Twitter screenshot)*

Take Twitter, which offers the ability to add image descriptions so that they will be included by screen readers. But the option is buried in its settings and not turned on by default.

"This dark pattern profoundly limits the ability of blind people to perceive and engage with memes, infographics, and photos that express identity, affect, and aesthetic experience," Ms. Fleet said.

Slowly, solutions do emerge. Google, for example, has introduced ReCAPTCHA, which attempts to determine human vs. bot based on the user's recent online interactions rather than making them click on pictures.

Who Makes the Rules?

Dr. Hollier looks at accessibility from two perspectives: Can people with disabilities access assistive technologies such as screen readers on the devices of their choice, and is online content accessible?

"What's been exciting in recent years is that whether we're talking Windows or iPhone, iPad or Android, or a Mac, accessibility features are largely built in," he said.

Ensuring content is accessible across desktops, laptops, tablets, and mobile devices, however, remains a challenge.

The Web Content Accessibility Guidelines 2.1 (WCAG 2.1) is an international standard, with recommendations that Dr Hollier said would address many of the digital "dark patterns."

He suggested moving Australian web sites and apps to WCAG 2.1 should be a priority.

Another challenge raised by Dr. Hollier is that Australia's Disability Discrimination Act, which was first passed in 1992, is not explicit enough about technological accessibility.

Issues of equal access to online information and services were raised in a landmark case brought by Bruce Maguire against the Sydney Organising Committee for the Olympic Games in 2000.

The committee was found to have unlawfully discriminated against Mr. Maguire, who is blind, for failing to provide a web site which was accessible, among other issues.

Dr. Ben Gauntlett, Australia's Disability Discrimination Commissioner, acknowledged the law was drafted at a time when most computer technologies were not prevalent.

"There is a critical need for us to assess whether the Disability Discrimination Act is fit for purpose in relation to new technology," he said.

"All service providers in Australia need to realize that there are a lot of people from a diverse range of backgrounds who use their services."

What to Do Next

To fight against "dark patterns" that stymy people with disabilities, advocates see a few ways forward.

Ms. Fleet suggested that accessibility errors could be displayed to users and developers just like spelling and grammar mistakes.

"Let's assume that users would rather know they're creating a problem, rather than 'save' them a moment on the assumption that no one will need their work to be accessible," she said.

"Treat accessibility errors like fire code violations: correct them every time so that the things we collectively build are safe for everyone."

Mr. Muscat said web accessibility should be a part of any project from the ground up.

"You can run all these tools and have these web accessibility inspectors...but the reality is, nothing beats the actual true user," he said.

Dr. Hollier also wants more people with disabilities involved in user experience testing, and Ms. Fleet suggested dark patterns arise because people who use accessibility tools are not on development teams or hired to test technology and new software before it goes live.

She believes that employing people with the lived experience of a disability can help but also advocates "fierce and sustained allyship to hold companies accountable to bake accessibility into ALL products."

"Tech culture—from platforms to procurement to education—must shift away from focusing on accessibility when a person with a disability presents a need, and shift toward treating accessibility as a consistently required part of every product," she said.[5]

By having some insight into frustrations of our users, we can always do better and improve on things. A large part of many creators' job is to balance business needs and user goals. When we can reduce friction and eliminate manipulative patterns, we are better able to serve our users.

Closing Thoughts

Do the best you can until you know better. Then when you know better, do better.

—Maya Angelou

There are some things here that Web Content Accessibility Guidelines does not cover; however, these best practices can be applied to keep all users engaged and avoid excluding individuals from using your products.

Here are some of the things we can do better to make things less annoying and more accessible:

- Clear calls to action: Clearly differentiate between buttons and links.

- Clear layout: Create the most logical layout for the individual users of the site.

- Typography: Use typography that is readable.

---

[5]The Internet thinks you're a robot, and other dark patterns people with disability face online www.abc.net.au/news/science/2019-07-13/dark-patterns-online-captcha-accessibility-disability-community/11301054

- Ability to apply filters: Allow individuals to control filters on the site.

- Clear navigation: Provide clear navigation so the individual knows where to go next.

- Appropriate related content: Ensure content is connected through the layout.

- Skip to content: Allow users to "skip to content" (this is especially helpful for screen readers).

- Correct contrast: Use color contrast checker to validate colors are within the guidelines.

CHAPTER 4

Compliance and Accessibility

Being compliant does not mean that you are accessible. When working on any site that is public facing, you will want to adhere to the Web Content Accessibility Guidelines (WCAG). Not only do you need to think about the web but also other digital experiences such as voice, augmented reality, virtual reality, and wearables.

One way to ensure accessibility is by following the WCAG. In 2018, the guidelines were updated. At the heart of WCAG are four main success areas: perceivable, operable, understandable, and robust, more commonly known as POUR. WCAG uses these categories for web accessibility. In this chapter, we will look at these key aspects of WCAG 2. But first, it's important to get a sense of what other legislation is in place to help with accessibility.

A Step in the Right Direction

In the past 15 years, both the United States and international governments have developed legislation to ensure equal rights for people with disabilities, including equivalent access to electronic and information technology.

© Regine M. Gilbert 2019
R. M. Gilbert, *Inclusive Design for a Digital World*,
https://doi.org/10.1007/978-1-4842-5016-7_4

Following is an overview of the various major standards and legislation pieces passed in various countries. This breakdown does not provide an exhaustive list of all such legislative pieces but does account for the majority of relevant standards and legislation.

United States

Rehabilitation Act

- Section 503—United States

- Section 504—United States

- Section 508—Section 508 of the Rehabilitation Act

Americans with Disabilities Act (ADA)
21st Century Communications and Video Accessibility Act (CVAA)

Other US Digital Accessibility Legislation

- Hearing Aid Compatibility Act

- NFB-NVA Certification Criteria—United States

- Air Carrier Access Act—United States

- State and Local Laws: An overview of state and local accessibility laws and standards compiled by Level Access

- State of California Code Section 11135

Canada

- Canadian Human Rights Act

- Accessibility for Ontarians with Disabilities Act

- Government of Canada Common Look and Feel Standards: The Government of Canada's Common Look and Feel Standards for public facing sites

Europe

- European Union

- Mandate M 376

- United Kingdom

- Germany

- Italy

- Netherlands

- Denmark

- Spain

- France

Asia Pacific

- Disability Discrimination Act—Australia

- Official Information Act and Human Rights Act—New Zealand

- Japanese Industrial Standard—Japan

International Standards

- Web Content Accessibility Guidelines 2.0

Further Reading

- WAI Policy Page: Provides a list of all the current international web accessibility standards

- ETSI Technical Report TR 102 612: Provides an overview of accessibility requirements relating to public sector procurement throughout the EU and the globe. By far the most detailed recent assessment of accessibility laws and standards.[1]

- WCAG 2.1 Highlights

- POUR: perceivable, operable, understandable, robust

- ADA's impact on Web

Web Content Accessibility Timeline

In 1999, the Web Accessibility Initiative (WAI) began with 14 Guidelines—65 priority checkpoints. When you think about the Web in 1999, it was completely different than it is today, and we didn't use cell phones the way we use them. Figure 4-1 provides a high-level view of nearly 20 years in the works.

---

[1]https://www.levelaccess.com/accessibility-regulations/

Figure 4-1. *Web Content Accessibility Guidelines*

Note that the Web Content Accessibility Guidelines are generally not something people print out to read, but WebAIM (`https://webaim.org/`) offers a great breakdown of WCAG, as well as the additional resources provided in the appendix.

POUR

The following sections provide an overview of POUR with examples.

Perceivable: Providing Text Alternatives

In 2018, Instagram, one of the most popular applications in the world, became a little more accessible by adding the option of custom alternative text so that individuals using screen readers could use Instagram. Figure 4-2 shows the option to add alt text.

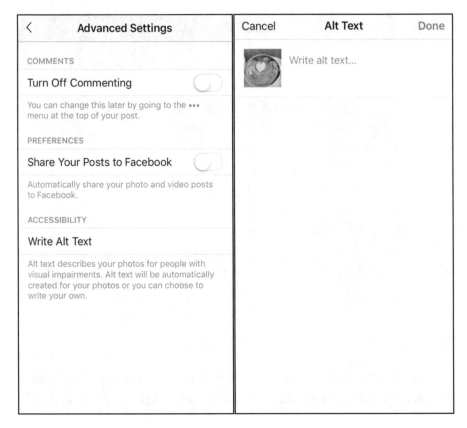

Figure 4-2. *Advanced settings to add alt text to Instagram images*

TRY IT YOURSELF

Alt text can be added to Instagram photos during the publishing process by following these steps:

- Start by taking a photo or uploading an existing photo to Instagram.

- Choose a filter and edit the image, and then tap Next.

- Tap Advanced Settings at the bottom of the screen.

- Tap Alt Text.

- Write your alt text in the box and tap Done.

Alt text can also be added to existing Instagram photos by following these steps.

- Go to the photo and tap the three-dot menu icon.

- Tap Add Alt Text in the bottom right.

- Write the alt text in the box and tap Done.

Captioning Options

Yahoo made a decision to apply WCAG to all of their videos by providing closed captioning and making accessibility a priority. They feel that all viewers are able to get the most out of videos when high-quality closed captions are applied. When Yahoo became a part of Oath, a Verizon company, they opened the door for individuals to provide feedback. Figure 4-3 shows Yahoo sports with closed captioning.

Figure 4-3. *Yahoo sports page with closed captioning*

Closed captioning is great when done properly; however, that is not always the case. For example, if you are using the closed captioning provided by YouTube, you will want to review the captions to make sure they are correct. The accuracy of YouTube's captions is dependent on speech recognition software which is not always accurate.

Closed Captioning Interview between 3PlayMedia and Brad Ellis of YouTube

3PlayMedia, a company specializing in captioning, spoke with Brad Ellis, a YouTube Product Manager at Google. Brad was able to break down captioning and why captioning is important.

Why caption?

Um, why *not* caption? Google thinks that all video material should be universally accessible, and introduced YouTube automatic captioning so that channels with users who do not upload their own captions will have some level of accessibility—though the consensus is, particularly among accessibility advocates, that auto captions are *not* accessible. Note also that YouTube's automatic captions *do not get indexed by Google* because they are so error prone. The only way for your captions to be indexed is to upload them yourself.

There are three really good reasons to caption: accessibility, searchability, and engagement.

- Accessible: 20% of Americans over age 12 experience significant enough hearing loss that it interferes with daily communication. Not captioning means that your videos are not accessible to 1/5 of your potential audience (in America, at least).

- Searchable: Also, Google and other search engines can't watch a video. Not captioning means that your videos can only be found based on their titles. What about all the incredible keywords and search terms you have in your video? Google has no idea about those.

- Engaging: At its core, captioning helps people understand more. If English is not your viewer's first language, they're more likely to follow if there are captions. Regardless, captions help all users engage more, which keeps them watching your video longer— which search engines reward in rankings.

Pros and Cons of Automatic Captioning

So, YouTube can caption videos automatically, right? Well, yes. As Brad said in our panel, automatic captions are there because "something is better than nothing." It's Google's way of providing at least a minimum level of captioning to all videos. YouTube's automatic captions tend to be pretty error prone, but they do provide some level of benefit (accuracy rates can be as high as 80% under good conditions and as poor as 50% under bad conditions). YouTube does allow users to edit their automated captions, which can improve accuracy a lot, but it takes time and effort. Basically, Brad suggested that the best use of their automatic captions is as a starting point for users to build higher-quality captions from.

Another option is to upload captions yourself, which YouTube lets you do quite easily. Uploading high-quality captions is the best option for creating highly accessible, searchable videos.

Speaking of, can you search for that?

Well, the bad news is that if you use YouTube's automatic captions for your video, Google/YouTube does not index them because of their inaccuracy rates. BUT the good news is that there is a way!

If you upload your own captions, Google will index them. That means that all of the content within your videos can suddenly be found!!!!

HIP HIP, HOORAY!!!!

Can you translate that for me?

Brad told us that 80% of views on YouTube come from outside the United States. WHOA. Does that give you an idea of how important captioning is? Without captions, it's much harder to translate! And if you don't translate, you're missing up to 4/5 of your potential audience. At the very least, captions help a lot for people whose first language is not English. Being able to read what is said in the video helps them understand it better.

Also, if you do add translations, your video will pop-up when people search for related content in a language other than English! Even better!

So, what should I do?

The main thing to get out of this is that basically, captioning your videos is really important. How you do that is your choice, but be aware that *YouTube's automated captions are not indexed by search engines* and might provide for some pretty humorous takes on your content. However, you can always go in and edit the automated captions to make them better.[2]

---

[2]Wondering What YouTube Has to Say About Captioning YouTube Videos? https://www.3playmedia.com/2014/04/04/wondering-youtube-say-captioning-youtube-videos/

If you are not familiar with the Closed Captioning option on YouTube, Figure 4-4 shows where the option is on the video player.

Figure 4-4. *Closed Captioning option on YouTube*

WCAG Success Criteria for captions

Specific Benefits of Success Criterion 1.2.2

- People who are deaf or have a hearing loss can access the auditory information in the synchronized media content through captions.

Examples of Success Criterion 1.2.2

- **A captioned tutorial**: A video clip shows how to tie a knot. The captions read, "(music) Using rope to tie knots was an important skill for the likes of sailors, soldiers and woodsmen." From *Sample Transcript Formatting* by Whit Anderson.

- A complex legal document contains synchronized media clips for different paragraphs that show a person speaking the contents of the paragraph. Each clip is associated with its corresponding paragraph. No captions are provided for the synchronized media.

- An instruction manual containing a description of a part and its necessary orientation is accompanied by a synchronized media clip showing the part in its correct orientation. No captions are provided for the synchronized media clip.

- An orchestra provides captions for videos of performances. In addition to capturing dialog and lyrics verbatim, captions identify nonvocal music by title, movement, composer, and any information that will help the user comprehend the nature of the audio. For instance, captions read, "[Orchestral Suite No. 3.2 in D major, BWV 1068, Air] [Johann Sebastian Bach, Composer] ♪ Calm melody with a slow tempo ♪" *Note:* Style guides for captions may differ among different languages.[3]

True Story—Podcast without Transcript

Sara Allen is deaf and wears a cochlear implant - here is her story.

Awesomely Luvvie and Glennon Doyle of "Momastery" are two fantastic bloggers that I follow religiously. They teamed up recently to produce a podcast about white privilege—topic that I was very interested in. I am hard of hearing and while I read lips very well, radio shows and podcasts have never been accessible to me. Much to my dismay, the podcast did not come with a transcription so I could not hear what they were talking about.

I wrote to the producers of the podcast and let them know that I was disappointed that I could not hear their podcast and that I hoped they would take measures to create a transcript so that I along with so many others could read along. I also let them know that it would be very good search engine optimization as their material would be searchable by Google.

---

[3]Captions (Prerecorded) https://www.w3.org/TR/UNDERSTANDING-WCAG20/media-equiv-captions.html

The author of Awesomely Luvvie received the feedback and immediately found a service to not only transcribe the current episode—she is continuing to transcribe her upcoming episodes. I messaged her a note of thanks to which she responded her own appreciation!

Captioning is something many people cannot live without and provides them an opportunity to view, learn, and be entertained on things that they could not engage with otherwise. Provided the option of captions makes your products more accessible overall.

Voice Recognition

Many people with disabilities use voice recognition technology which enables them to work, shop, order food, and many other things. Today you can speak to your computer, phone, or other digital devices.

What is "voice recognition"?

Voice recognition can be used for dictating text in a form field, as well as navigating to and activating links, buttons, and other controls. Most computers and mobile devices today have built-in voice recognition functionality. Some voice recognition tools allow complete control over computer interaction, allowing the user to scroll the screen, copy and paste text, activate menus, and perform other functions.

Who depends on this feature?

- People with physical disabilities who cannot use the keyboard or mouse.

- People with chronic conditions, such as repetitive stress injuries (RSI), who need to limit or avoid using the keyboard or mouse.

- People with cognitive and learning disabilities who need to use voice rather than to type.

What are the additional benefits?

- Content works for people with temporary limitations, such as a broken arm.

- Content is more usable for people who prefer to speak rather than type, for example, while multitasking.

What needs to happen for this to work?

Content must be properly designed and coded so that it can be controlled by voice. Keyboard compatibility is the basis for such coding. In addition, labels and identifiers for controls in the source code need to match their visual presentation, so that it is clear which voice command will activate a control.[4]

Operable: Components and Navigation

Keyboard Accessibility

Keyboard accessibility is for those who only use keyboards to find their way through a site. Many people use keyboard shortcuts when creating screenshots or if they want to copy and paste something. Keyboard accessibility is important for people who may use assistive technologies, individuals with motor disabilities, and people who are super-users of keyboards. Figure 4-5 shows some shortcuts on a Mac using the Chrome browser.

---

[4]Voice Recognition https://www.w3.org/WAI/perspective-videos/voice/

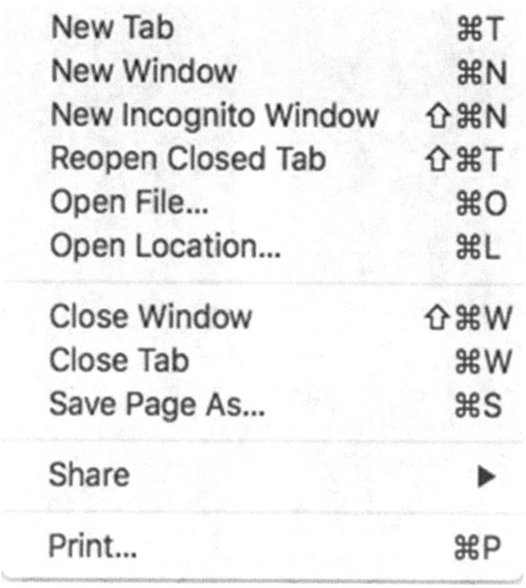

New Tab	⌘T
New Window	⌘N
New Incognito Window	⇧⌘N
Reopen Closed Tab	⇧⌘T
Open File...	⌘O
Open Location...	⌘L
Close Window	⇧⌘W
Close Tab	⌘W
Save Page As...	⌘S
Share	▶
Print...	⌘P

Figure 4-5. *Chrome "File Tab"; there are various shortcuts for a Mac keyboard*

As creators, it's important to keep in mind that someone may only be using a keyboard to navigate through our site. If creating a site, try not to make things that only someone with a mouse can use.

Gestures

Gestures have been added in the updates to WCAG 2.1. Many of us use smart phones and many of us use gestures to interact with our phones. Gestures include swiping, double taps, and long press.

To open an iPhone 6s, an individual may do a long press in order to unlock their phone (see Figure 4-6) and they may shake their phone to undo typing.

 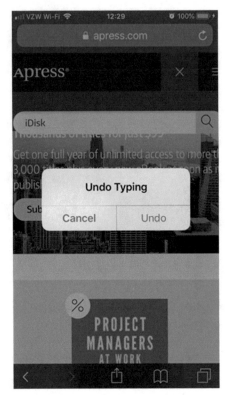

Figure 4-6. iPhone 6s' screens showing home screen. Users can gesture a long press to unlock home screen and shake to undo typing

Gestures are gaining even more prominence as we increase our use of gesture-based technologies. You rarely see people without their phones in their hands these days. Keeping an idea of how people use gestures on a day-to-day basis will help further improve experiences for individuals.

Provide Users with Enough Time to Complete a Task

Another operable feature is giving users enough time to complete a task. An example of this is Ticketmaster and purchasing a ticket. At the top they provide you with the amount of time that you have left to purchase your ticket. In Figure 4-7, the upper right-hand corner shows the minutes and seconds left to buy the tickets.

Figure 4-7. *Ticketmaster web site shows time left to purchase a ticket is 4 minutes and 52 seconds*

Understandable: Error Identification

We have all been there, we fill out a form, and then we can't move forward. Error states occur when things go wrong and the users may or may not receive notification of the error. Figure 4-8 shows an example of how to make errors understandable. In this instance, it shows a password may not be recognized.

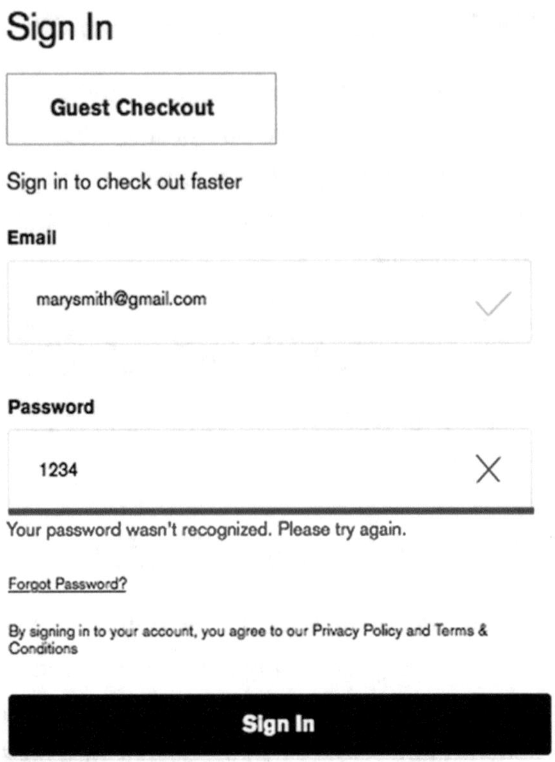

Sign In

Guest Checkout

Sign in to check out faster

Email

marysmith@gmail.com

Password

1234

Your password wasn't recognized. Please try again.

Forgot Password?

By signing in to your account, you agree to our Privacy Policy and Terms & Conditions

Sign In

Figure 4-8. Error state for password on a sign in page

Consider the various states in which your users might encounter errors and provide the best options for them. The best way to handle error states is to plan for them through design and execution.

Robust

A robust product means it is compatible for all types of assistive technologies. Ask yourself: "Is your site compatible with assistive technologies like screen readers or screen magnification software?" If not, it isn't robust enough, and as a result, you'll exclude some individuals from using your product.

Figure 4-9. *Assistive technology* `https://comcastnewsmakers.com/`
`Videos/2018/10/4/Latest-Trends-in-Assistive-Technology`

ADA's Impact on Web Accessibility

In the United States, the laws around web accessibility have historically been ambiguous. In 1990, the American with Disabilities Act was passed and applied to prohibit discrimination to people with disabilities in all areas of public life.

In 1990 when the ADA was passed, the Internet was around, but no one was using it the way we use it today. There have been several attempts at passing legislation in relation to web accessibility; however, none have passed.

Over the past 15 years, there has been an increase in accessibility lawsuits. Meaning, individuals and organizations have pursued litigation for the inaccessibility of web sites. And From 2017 to 2018, web accessibility lawsuits increased by 181%. While the sudden uptake in lawsuits is alarming, it serves as a wakeup call for companies.[5] The Internet is becoming an undeniable necessity; it's important that everyone has equal access to it.

In an effort to understand how the ADA has impacted web accessibility lawsuits, let's go over some of the lawsuits.

Target 2008[6]

Target settled a class action lawsuit with the National Federation of the Blind over accessibility complaints with Target.com. Despite the law being unclear as to whether the Americans with Disabilities Act (ADA) applies to web sites, the company will pay a substantial fee and update its web site to make it accessible to the blind.

Harvard and MIT 2015[7]

In 2015, Harvard and MIT were sued for violating anti-discrimination laws by failing to provide closed captioning in online lectures, courses, podcasts, and other educational materials.

---

[5]Web Accessibility Lawsuits www.3playmedia.com/2019/06/12/2018sweb-accessibility-lawsuits/

[6]Target to pay $6 million to settle site accessibility suit
https://arstechnica.com/uncategorized/2008/08/
target-to-pay-6-million-to-settle-site-accessibility-suit/

[7]Higher Education Lawsuites https://www.csusm.edu/accessibility/ati/
lawsuits/index.html

Winn Dixie 2017[8]

One of the most important cases in recent years was the lawsuit against Winn Dixie. This particular case used the American with Disabilities Act as the basis for the claim. Because the ADA is a federal law, it opened up the door for people to follow the law in regard to the creation and development of web sites.

This verdict and order is especially significant, as this is the first federal court to hold a full trial regarding web site accessibility as it relates to the ADA and visually impaired users, to make findings of fact, to effectively adopt the WCAG 2.0 standard as the measure of a compliant web site, and to award a detailed injunction.

This decision, particularly in light of its adoption of the WCAG 2.0 standard, will impact the way businesses think about compliance and risk mitigation.

Beyoncé—Parkwood Entertainment 2019[9]

A class action lawsuit claims that Beyoncé's official web site violates the Americans with Disabilities Act (1990) by denying visually impaired users equal access to its products and services, according to the Hollywood Reporter.

Web accessibility requires photos to be coded with alt text so that screen readers used by visually impaired users can speak the alternative text. Dan Shaked, attorney for plaintiff Mary Conner, said: "There are

---

[8]First Federal Trial on Website Accessibility: Winn-Dixie Violates ADA https://www.fredlaw.com/news__media/2017/06/14/1548/ first_federal_trial_on_website_accessibility_winn-dixie_violates_ada/

[9]Beyoncé's Parkwood Entertainment sued over website accessibility https://www.theguardian.com/music/2019/jan/04/beyonce-parkwood-entertainment-sued-over-website-accessibility

many important pictures on beyonce.com that lack a text equivalent... As a result, Plaintiff and blind beyonce.com customers are unable to determine what is on the web site, browse the web site, or investigate and/or make purchases."

Conclusion

"Whether we're incorporating accessibility as a preventative measure to a lawsuit, fostering innovation, or rounding out our design and development toolkits, we're helping people participate more fully in the digital landscape." Erin Newby - Accessibility Advocate.

The American with Disabilities Act has been used as a way of compliance for the web and may continue to do so until there are laws in place that apply to digital experiences relatated to accessibility. At the end of the day, the more people that have access to your products the better. The goal is to create a POUR web site and not a poor web site. POUR stands for perceivable, operable, understandable, and robust.

For best results, consult a professional accessibility expert who can give you audit of your work with recommendation on how to fix any errors. Accessibility plugins and web/mobile checkers may catch some errors but not all of them. There is no substitute for an expert who can examine your site in detail and provide a proper audit. Continue learning and improving to make sure the maximum number of people have access to your products.

CHAPTER 5

Building a Vision for the Future: Design Strategies for Accessibility

We may not always think this way but user experience starts the moment a project begins. We start asking questions and researching W5H (who, what, where, when, why, and how). Design is a way of thinking, and as such, we must approach our project with an open mind.

The beauty of user experience is that it is platform agnostic, meaning you can approach any digital or physical product and use similar strategies.

As creators, we help our users focus on their core tasks for our products, such as: What features do they need to accomplish their goals? What are the goals of the business? How do we align business needs and user goals?

In this chapter, we will discuss design frameworks, principles for accessibility, and creating accessible content that can assist in making more inclusive experiences for individuals using your digital products.

© Regine M. Gilbert 2019
R. M. Gilbert, *Inclusive Design for a Digital World*,
https://doi.org/10.1007/978-1-4842-5016-7_5

User Experience Starts the Moment a Project Begins

Figure 5-1 is a framework created by James Vanié and Regine Gilbert.

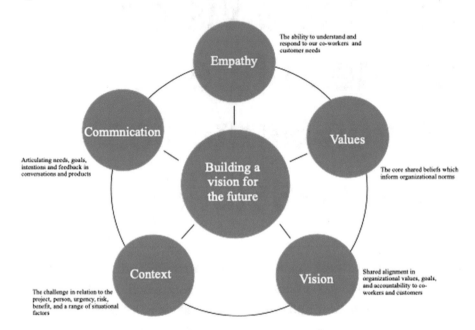

Figure 5-1. *EVVCC Framework by James Vanié and Regine Gilbert[1]*

A house without a frame cannot stand on its own. One way of looking at a framework is to see it as the supportive approach to designing products. Frameworks can provide structure around how you might approach certain problems. In the EVVCC framework, the approach is to look at projects with an informed lens. The EVVCC stands for empathy, values, vision, context, and communication.

---

[1]Figure 5-1 EVVCC Framework by James Vanié and Regine Gilbert originally presented in the talk "The Future Depends on You: The importance of informed design"

The framework is broken down into five areas:

- Empathy: The ability to understand and respond to our co-workers and customer needs

- Values: The core shared beliefs which inform organizational norms

- Vision: Shared alignment in organizational values, goals, and accountability to co-workers and customers

- Context: The challenge in relation to the project, person, urgency, risk, benefit, and a range of situational factors

- Communication: Articulating needs, goals, intentions, and feedback in conversations and products

Having a framework could put everyone on the same page. Whether you are a startup or an established business, it takes a team to build great products. Part of working to achieve Inclusive Design starts with having an idea of who you are serving and who you could possibly be excluding.

> *Exclusion is not a PR-friendly word, but it is a universal human experience. We all know how it feels when we're left out.*
>
> — Kat Holmes, *Mismatch Design*

People say that they can't think of all the disabilities out there and they cannot address all of their users. This is often times true; there is no way to address all the needs of the people using your products. If you can't consider all disabilities, consider blindness. About 80% of accessibility issues are related to blindness.[2]

---

[2]Interaction Design Foundation https://www.interaction-design.org/literature/article/10-principles-of-accessibility

With that said, by thinking about accessibility from the start, you are already ahead by incorporating thought about all possible users of your products.

In the EVVCC framework, you start with empathy and the vision and values of your organization. Another piece of the framework is communication and context. There is no one-size-fits-all solution, and the context of the situation may vary depending on the needs of the business as well as your users. What is the overall goal for the product and are you addressing your users' needs in correlation to that?

Design strategy is pivotal when producing and developing a product. It's not something that everyone may have at the start of a project. However, it can serve the project well when it is done well.

Once a way of working has been established, it may be good for some teams or individuals to think about the principles for accessibility.

AirBnb and News Deeply Case Study

There are many types of frameworks to consider: Airbnb uses Another Lens frameworks for creations—a research tool for conscious creatives.

How can you design for everyone without understanding the full picture?

To help examine how bias influences our worldview, Airbnb Design partnered with News Deeply, a journalism startup dedicated to providing in-depth coverage of the world's most critical challenges. The end result was the Shadow to Light installation, an experience that pressed us to recognize our biases and grapple with our limitations.

We believe that both designers and journalists have the responsibility to shine a light on their bias by asking the right questions, seeking conflicting viewpoints, and expanding their lens to build inclusive, global solutions.

Three Guiding Principles

Together with News Deeply, our design research team put together a set of guiding principles and exercises: balancing your bias, considering the opposite, and embracing a growth mindset. These help designers address skewed perspectives in order to create thoughtful, inclusive work.

Our tool, Another Lens, poses a set of questions to help you balance your bias, consider the opposite, and embrace a growth mindset. Figures 5-2 through 5-4 show imagery for balancing your bias, considering the opposite, and embracing a growth mindset.

Figure 5-2. Balance your bias

Figure 5-3. Consider the opposite

Figure 5-4. Embrace a growth mindset

Here are some of the questions, two from each area—balance your bias, consider the opposite, and embrace a growth mindset.

Balance Your Bias

Question: What are my lenses?

Background

Your lenses are always there, and they influence how you see the world. These could be inherited (e.g., race, gender, nationality), developed (political views or religious perspectives), or behavioral (How do you approach problems? Whom do you get advice from? Where do you find news?). Everyone has lenses, but not everyone is aware that they do or even what they are. Be explicit about the lenses you apply to any given decision or project. As you work to identify your own lenses, also think through the lenses you might be missing.

Question: Am I just confirming my assumptions, or am I challenging them?

Background

Confirmation bias is the tendency to search for, interpret, favor, and remember information in a way that confirms one's existing beliefs. It's very much a human tendency and is particularly strong around issues that are emotionally charged. It's also one of the biggest threats to equitable design and fair reporting. If we seek to confirm or validate an idea, we will certainly be able to do so. As designers, we must constantly examine our own biases and be honest with ourselves about how our own lenses could bring imbalance to the projects we pursue, the sources we talk to, and the language we use. Write down three things about your background that might be informing your work, and for each thing, write down a corresponding assumption that might lead to bias.[3]

Consider the Opposite

Question: What would the world look like if my assumptions were wrong?

---

[3]Another Lens https://airbnb.design/anotherlens/

Background

Back in the 1980s, psychologist Charles Lord ran an experiment to try and help people overcome confirmation bias—the trick our minds play on us that causes us to highlight information that already confirms what we believe and ignore information that disproves it. He and his colleagues were able to show that asking people explicitly to "consider the opposite" had a direct impact on overcoming confirmation bias. Never ask questions to validate—work to disprove your assumptions instead. The next time you design a solution, first write down your assumptions and your hypotheses; then write down what you'd see in the world if your assumptions were wrong. Any research you do to inform your work should be focused on helping to find evidence of those things.

Question: Who might disagree with what I'm designing?

Background

We tend to surround ourselves with people who are similar to us—this is called homophily. It's simply part of human nature; hundreds of studies have been conducted that illustrate how similarity fosters connection. When designing, make sure that you gather input on your solutions not only from people who are similar to you (i.e., your friends and family) but also from those with a wildly different point of view.

Embrace a Growth Mindset

Question: Is my audience open to change?

Background

In a "fixed mindset," people believe that they have a set of fixed, immovable traits and their experiences reinforce these traits. In a "growth mindset," people believe that their traits and abilities can be developed and improved upon, and their experiences are opportunities to learn and become more resilient. How people react to change—whether they're open to it or resist it—is very much dependent on which mindset they subscribe to. Ensure your design works both for people with a fixed mindset and people with a growth mindset by working to understand where people are and then meeting them there.

Question: If I could learn one thing to help me on this project, what would that one thing be?

Background

By focusing time on learning, we also end up creating space to shake bias out of our thinking. Research shows that when people are distracted or overwhelmed, they tend to rely on biases even more. Make sure you've carved out time for learning, not just doing, on this project.

It can help to go beyond looking into your industry to find answers for approaching problems as Airbnb did in this case study by reaching out to the journalism community for answers to questions of bias. More questions can be found on the website `https://airbnb.design/anotherlens/#answer15`.

Principles for Inclusivity

Design may start with a brand-new product or iterating on an old one. Wherever you are in the process, it may be good to look at what could be done to keep the people you are creating the product at the forefront of your team's minds.

Here are some great tips from the Paciello group for inclusive design:[4]

- Provide a comparable experience.

- Consider situation.

- Be consistent.

- Give control.

- Offer choice.

- Prioritize content.

- Add value.

When incorporating accessibility into your product, you want them to have a comparable experience to those who may be using assistive technologies.

At the end of the day, we want to make sure users of all abilities are able to complete their goals with our products. Asking the question "What value are we providing?" to both the business and the user with whatever we are building can lead to larger adoption of the use of the product. That is when we are actually providing value to both the business and the user.

Design Tips for More Inclusive Designs

Table 5-1 shows the Do's and Don'ts of Inclusive Design, published by UK.Gov.[5] You can use this as a reminder of what to consider when building your project or as a checklist to ensure you've kept your development project as inclusive as possible.

---

[4]Paciello Group Inclusive Design Principles `https://developer.paciellogroup.com/blog/2017/06/inclusive-design-principles/`

[5]Gov.UK Accessibility blog `https://accessibility.blog.gov.uk/2016/09/02/dos-and-donts-on-designing-for-accessibility/`

Table 5-1. *Do's and Don'ts of Inclusive Design*

Designing for users	Do	Don't
on the autistic spectrum	use simple colors write in plain English use simple sentences and bullets make buttons descriptive—for example, Attach files **build simple and consistent layouts**	use bright contrasting colors use figures of speech and idioms create a wall of text make buttons vague and unpredictable—for example, Click here **build complex and cluttered layouts**
of screen readers	describe images and provide transcripts for video follow a linear, logical layout structure content using HTML5 build for keyboard use only **write descriptive links and heading—for example, Contact us**	only show information in an image or video spread content all over a page rely on text size and placement for structure force mouse or screen use **write uninformative links and heading—for example, Click here**

(*continued*)

Table 5-1. (*continued*)

Designing for users	Do	Don't
with low vision	use good contrasts and a readable font size	use low color contrasts and small font size
	publish all information on web pages (HTML)	bury information in downloads
	use a combination of color, shapes, and text	only use color to convey meaning
	follow a linear, logical layout and ensure text flows and is visible when text is magnified to 200%	spread content all over a page and force user to scroll horizontally when text is magnified to 200%
	put buttons and notifications in context	**separate actions from their context**
with physical or motor disabilities	make large clickable actions	demand precision
	give form fields space	bunch interactions together
	design for keyboard or speech-only use	make dynamic content that requires a lot of mouse movement
	design with mobile and touch screen in mind	have short time-out windows
	provide shortcuts	**tire users with lots of typing and scrolling**

(*continued*)

Table 5-1. (*continued*)

Designing for users	Do	Don't
who are D/deaf or hard of hearing	write in plain English use subtitles or provide transcripts for video use a linear, logical layout break up content with subheadings, images, and videos **let users ask for their preferred communication support when booking appointments**	use complicated words or figures of speech put content in audio or video only make complex layouts and menus make users read long blocks of content **don't make telephone the only means of contact for users**
with dyslexia	use images and diagrams to support text align text to the left and keep a consistent layout consider producing materials in other formats (e.g., audio and video) keep content short, clear, and simple let users change the contrast between background and text	use large blocks of heavy text underline words, use italics, or write capitals force users to remember things from previous pages– give reminders and prompts rely on accurate spelling— use autocorrect or provide suggestions put too much information in one place

This is a great list from the UK.Gov on some do's and don'ts. This list is not meant to be strict guidelines but a roadmap for what to look out for when creating digital products. Besides trying out some of the design principles, you will want to test them out before any release. In Chapter 9, we will discuss more in relation to usability testing products with people with disabilities.

At the heart of any digital product is what it can offer to the users. When it comes to what we crave, the most is enjoyable content. Designing accessible content is part of what can make for a more inclusive experience when done right.

Designing Accessible Content

Accessible content should be simple—KIS (keep it simple). An example of keeping it simple is by having a "Skip to Content" link. Figure 5-5 "Skip to Content" link allows users to go directly to the content they are looking for instead of going through a bunch of things they may have no interest in. Upon entry to a web site, a keyboard user might select the tab key on their keyboard. One of the first things they encounter when coming to the site is "Skip to Content". This works well for assistive technology users as well as keyboard users to better navigate the page.

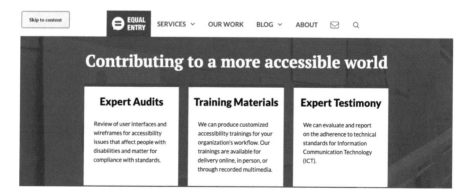

Figure 5-5. *Equal Entry web site yellow "Skip to Content" button at top of page* https://equalentry.com/

Accessible Writing

In the spirit of KIS, use writing that is not complex. Here are a few tips for accessible writing:

- Use simple words.

- Be concise with calls to action.

- Keep sentences short (think about Tweets-short and full of information).

- Do not use style of font as the only indicator.

Another important accessibility factor to keep in mind is that screen readers have font limitations. Here is a list of font formatting that cannot be recognized by screen readers:

- Strikethroughs

- Bold

- Color

- Bold

- Italics

- Underline

Use other types of indicators to signify importance.

Provide guidance to your users so that they can move throughout your site and on to the next thing in order to accomplish their goal. And you want to do that in the simplest way possible.

You never know where someone may be when accessing your product or what types of technology they may be using. For example, if someone is using a screen reader and they are not able to visually see the image, alt text can provide them with a description of what that image is. If someone is in an area with low bandwidth and the image is unable to download, the alternative text could tell them what the image is. Figure 5-6 shows an example of HTML code for alternative images.

```
<img src="image.jpg" alt="image description" title="image tooltip"/>
```

Figure 5-6. *HTML image tag*

Provide Enough Time to Use and Read Content

> *The designer should assume that people will be interrupted during their activities.*
>
> — The Design of Everyday Things[6]

Providing users with enough time to use and read content will give them time to complete their task; it may also add anxiety to users who may not be able to complete things in a timely manner. Be sure to provide more time to complete tasks. Figure 5-7 shows a timer in the right-hand corner with the amount of time left to purchase a concert ticket.

In our ever-distracting world, it's good to give more than enough time because often times people are distracted and tend to come back to things after a short or long while.

---

[6]*Design of Everyday Things* Don Norman. Basic Books

Figure 5-7.   Ticket purchase timer https://winnipegfolkfestival. frontgatetickets.com/event/aq0zldopnq22q0br

Conclusion

We live in a world where all of us are temporarily able bodied, and it pays to make more inclusive products, not only for others but also for ourselves.

Design principles and frameworks are just a start and can lead to you and your team finding an impactful way to create more inclusive and accessible experiences. Asking questions of yourself and your team can help you get to asking the right questions for building your products and making your products more inclusive.

There is no one-size-fits-all scenario, so it is recommended that you customize these guides based on your current working situation. In the end, we want to add value to the use of our products by having the widest audience possible. On our internal teams, we have a chance to create spaces for allowing more people to use our products when we incorporate accessibility early on.

We are on our way to building a vision for the future, not just our future users but our future selves.

CHAPTER 6

Inclusive Design Research

Inclusive design is good business.

—IBM founder Thomas John Watson Jr.

The case for doing research and incorporating accessibility into your plans early will benefit your organization. Not only can your organization benefit from incorporating people with disabilities when testing a product, you can also benefit by making them a part of the process from the very start. Involving people with disabilities in product development and advertisement can help businesses access a market worth billions of dollars.[1]

Ultimately, the decision on how to move forward with the project will be the responsibility of the stakeholders involved. Stakeholders may include executive leadership, managers, product owners, and so on.

In the building of digital experiences, we have to remember that human beings are going to be the ones using our products. It is easy to get wrapped up into our products and what they can do and we sometimes forget that.

---

[1]Meeting the Needs of Adults with Disabilities `https://www.air.org/news/press-release/meeting-needs-adults-disabilities-marketplace` accessed on April 3, 2019

© Regine M. Gilbert 2019
R. M. Gilbert, *Inclusive Design for a Digital World*,
https://doi.org/10.1007/978-1-4842-5016-7_6

Everyone is capable of doing research no matter what your role is on the team. One of the balancing acts that people have to weigh is business needs vs. user goals. Research can help balance things out by asking questions and seeking answers. Research plans can help facilitate the process.

One of the first questions I recommend asking is, "What problem are we solving?" If this is not something you can answer, you may want to reconsider what you are working on. As creators in this digital age, we should be making things better for people and help them solve problems. After asking what problem you are solving, move forward with a research plan. Research plans can vary depending on what is needed for a project.

In Table 6-1, we can see an example of what a research plan could include and some questions you might ask. Incorporating accessibility into the research plan will provide you with forethought and not leave accessibility as an afterthought after a product is developed.

Table 6-1. *Example of research plan—pick and choose what works for you and your products needs*

Research plan purpose	What is the purpose of the research? What goals are you trying to achieve?
Context of use of the product	Is this an existing product in which the uses are known? Is this a new product? When and where will people be using the product?
Priority areas of research	Based on your goals, what are the priority areas for your research?
Methodologies	What methodologies will you use for your research? Personas? Interviews? Surveys? Usability Testing? Others?
Premortem (what could go wrong)	Make a list of all the things that could go wrong during research and make a plan to mitigate those risks

(continued)

Table 6-1. (*continued*)

Timeframe	How much time do you have for research and synthesis?
Research questions	What type of questions could you ask that will help you reach the goal of your research?
Goals	What is the primary goal of the research? How does this align with business goals?
Participants	Who will your participants be? How will you include people with disabilities? How will you recruit participants?
Script?	If the users are testing a product with a goal in mind, what type of script will you use?
Ethics	What are the ethical values of your organization?

Recruiting People with Disabilities

Included in your research plan will include how you plan to include participants. Getting people with disabilities involved in the process requires reaching out to local communities or using services that can help you find participants. The people you recruit should be people who use your product and are a part of your target market. Think about goal of the project when recruiting participants.

Focus the Recruiting Strategy

If you work with an external recruiter, ask them if they have experience recruiting people with disabilities; some do. If you are recruiting internally (without an external recruiter), you may need to reach out to organizations that have access to people with disabilities. For example, if you need to recruit participants with visually disabilities in the United States, you should contact a local chapter of the National Federation of the Blind (https://nfb.org/state-and-local-organizations) or a local training center such as the Carroll Center for the Blind in Massachusetts (`http://carroll.org/`). If you use social media to advertise your study, a good approach is to use the hashtag #a11y (stands for accessibility—there are 11 letters between the "a" and "y") in your post.[2] Other organizations for people with disabilities are listed in the appendix.

Remember that you want to gather enough information to make informed decisions.

Exclusion

Design is much more likely to be the source of exclusion than inclusion. When we design for other people, our own biases and preferences often lead the way. When we create a solution that we, ourselves, can see, touch, understand, or hear, it tends to work well for people with similar circumstances or preferences to us. It also ends up excluding many more people.

This is especially true with respect to disability. The World Health Organization defines disability as a mismatched interaction between the features of a person's body and the features of the environment in which they live. This is also known as the social definition, or model, of disability.[3]

From the start, you can think about who you are excluding. Far too many times, people with disabilities are left out of research. The research plan and the time that you may have to plan will vary depending on the size of the project. The types of research you will want to conduct will vary in relation to what the goals of the research are.

---

[2]Tips for conducting usability studies with participants with disabilities `www.smashingmagazine.com/2018/03/tips-conducting-usability-studies-participants-disabilities/`

[3]What we are leaving out of the discussion around design `https://eyeondesign.aiga.org/what-were-leaving-out-of-the-discussion-around-inclusive-design/`

Discovering how and why people behave as they do and what opportunities that presents for your business or organization will open the way to more innovative and appropriate design solutions than asking how they feel or merely tweaking your current design based on analytics.[4]

There are several types of methodologies you can use when researching your products. The great thing about research is that you can apply it to any platform. Christian Rohrer has a great layout of the landscape of research methodologies listing out attitudinal vs. behavioral and qualitative vs. quantitative (see Figure 6-1). We'll discuss the differences between the types of research and what might be best depending on the context of what you are researching.

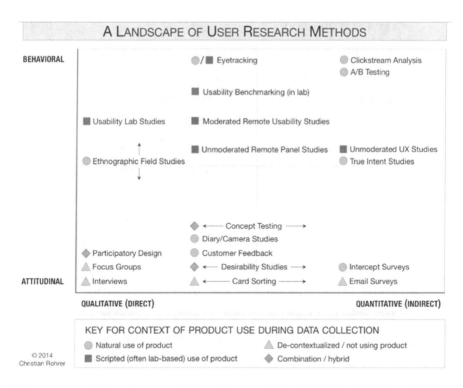

Figure 6-1. *A Landscape of User Research Methods by Christian Rohrer*

---

[4]*Just Enough Research*. Erika Hall. A Book Apart

20 UX Research Methods in Brief

Here's a short description of the user research methods shown in the preceding chart:

- **Usability Lab Studies**: Participants are brought into a lab, one-on-one with a researcher, and given a set of scenarios that lead to tasks and usage of specific interest within a product or service.

- **Ethnographic Field Studies**: Researchers meet with and study participants in their natural environment, where they would most likely encounter the product or service in question.

- **Participatory Design**: Participants are given design elements or creative materials in order to construct their ideal experience in a concrete way that expresses what matters to them most and why.

- **Focus Groups**: Groups of 3–12 participants are led through a discussion about a set of topics, giving verbal and written feedback through discussion and exercises.

- **Interviews**: A researcher meets with participants one-on-one to discuss in depth what the participant thinks about the topic in question.

- **Eyetracking**: An eyetracking device is configured to precisely measure where participants look as they perform tasks or interact naturally with web sites, applications, physical products, or environments.

- **Usability Benchmarking**: Tightly scripted usability studies are performed with several participants, using precise and predetermined measures of performance.

- **Moderated Remote Usability Studies**: Usability studies conducted remotely with the use of tools such as screen-sharing software and remote-control capabilities.

- **Unmoderated Remote Panel Studies**: A panel of trained participants who have video recording and data collection software installed on their own personal devices uses a web site or product while thinking aloud, having their experience recorded for immediate playback and analysis by the researcher or company.

- **Concept Testing**: A researcher shares an approximation of a product or service that captures the key essence (the value proposition) of a new concept or product in order to determine if it meets the needs of the target audience; it can be done one-on-one or with larger numbers of participants and either in person or online.

- **Diary/Camera Studies**: Participants are given a mechanism (diary or camera) to record and describe aspects of their lives that are relevant to a product or service, or simply core to the target audience; diary studies are typically longitudinal and can only be done for data that is easily recorded by participants.

- **Customer Feedback**: Open-ended and/or close-ended information provided by a self-selected sample of users, often through a feedback link, button, form, or email.

- **Desirability Studies**: Participants are offered different visual-design alternatives and are expected to associate each alternative with a set of attributes selected from a closed list; these studies can be both qualitative and quantitative.

- **Card Sorting**: A quantitative or qualitative method that asks users to organize items into groups and assign categories to each group. This method helps create or refine the information architecture of a site by exposing users' mental models.

- **Clickstream Analysis**: Analyzing the record of screens or pages that users click and see, as they use a site or software product; it requires the site to be instrumented properly or the application to have telemetry data collection enabled.

- **A/B Testing** (also known as "multivariate testing," "live testing," or "bucket testing"): A method of scientifically testing different designs on a site by randomly assigning groups of users to interact with each of the different designs and measuring the effect of these assignments on user behavior.

- **Unmoderated UX Studies**: A quantitative or qualitative and automated method that uses a specialized research tool to capture participant behaviors (through software installed on participant computers/browsers) and attitudes (through embedded survey questions), usually by giving participants goals or scenarios to accomplish with a site or prototype.

- **True Intent Studies**: A method that asks random site visitors what their goal or intention is upon entering the site, measures their subsequent behavior, and asks whether they were successful in achieving their goal upon exiting the site.

- **Intercept Surveys**: A survey that is triggered during the use of a site or application.

- **Email Surveys**: A survey in which participants are recruited from an email message.[5]

Generative Research vs. Evaluative Research

When generating research, you may be conducting interviews, surveys, usability studies, etc. You are working to answer the question of what problem you are solving for. You are gathering data to be used to make informed decisions on what to do next.

Evaluative research is when you focus on the purpose of your product and may involve usability testing. Usability testing will be detailed in Chapter 8.

REAL-LIFE CASE STUDY: DIGITAL SERVICES GEORGIA

Scope: Accessibility, Visual Design
Timeline: June 2015–January 2016
Members: Nikhil Deshpande, Kendra Skeene, Jenna Tollerson, Jasmyne Dove
More and more, people turn to the Internet for critical information. Today, important government information and services—unemployment benefits, veterans' services, tax information, and so much more—are available online. But can everyone access it?

More than 8% of Georgia residents under the age of 65 have some form of disability, and the percentage only increases when you look at older groups. At the same time, people over 65 are the fastest growing group of Internet users. This is often the population that benefits most from online services and information but only when they can access it!

---

[5]When to use which user-experience research methods www.nngroup.com/articles/which-ux-research-methods/

How We Made the Digital Services Georgia Platform More Accessible Case Study

So what did we actually do to make the platform more accessible? Advised by AMAC and the ADA's office, we made the following changes to the platform code:

- **Increased Color Contrast**

  Text needs to contrast with its background enough for users with low vision and color blindness to be able to read it. Previously, some of the text in our themes had too low of contrast to pass WCAG 2.0 AA standards. We used WebAIM Contrast Checker to narrow down our theme colors and select only accessible combinations for text and background colors.

- **Better Font Legibility**

  We knew from the beginning that certain fonts are easier to read than others. When we took a second look at our theme fonts from an accessibility-focused perspective, we realized that some of our header and navigation fonts could be easier to read.

- **Improved Semantic Markup**

  A lot of the accessibility needs can be addressed simply by using semantic markup—that is, using HTML markup that describes what content is and does instead of relying on styled <div> or <span> tags for everything. By adjusting our use of heading tags for all heading levels, removing heading tags from non-heading content, and adding <label> tags to the search form, we made our web sites more accessible and more SEO-friendly.

- **Improved Keyboard-Only Navigation**
  Sometimes, users need to navigate the Web with a keyboard, rather than a mouse or touch screen. We adjusted our semantic markup to make content easier to access when navigating solely with a keyboard or screen reader software. Some of these changes included adding a visible border around all links when a user tabs to them (called a "visible focus"), adding labels to form elements, and making the menus easier to tab through.

- **Enhanced Functionality for Screen Readers**
  For certain elements, we enhanced the screen reader experience with ARIA labels. Examples included adding ARIA accessibility labeling to "Read More" links across the platform to provide additional context to the link for screen reader users and adding ARIA labeling to pagination links to provide more context for where each "Next" or "Back" link goes.

Before and After

Subtle, not huge changes were made to the themes' visual appearance, as shown in Figures 6-2 through 6-7.

Figure 6-2. *Before (Classic 2 theme)*

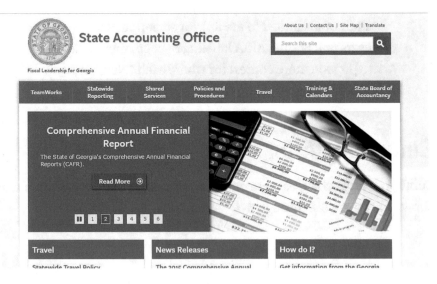

Figure 6-3. *After (Classic 2 theme)*

Figure 6-4. *Before (Friendly theme)*

Figure 6-5. *After (Friendly theme)*

Figure 6-6. *Before (Portal theme)*

Figure 6-7. *After (Portal theme)*

Accessibility for All

With these improvements, state agency web sites on our platform now have accessible themes. We've also built accessibility into our process for designing and building new platform features to ensure that all future development meets our standards from the start. However, the agency content managers play a critical role in ensuring the site's information is also accessible.[6]

Georgia's way of addressing accessibility through planning and research helped them build a better and more inclusive product.

Here are nine steps of user research from Erika Hall of Mule Design:

1. Get comfortable being uncomfortable.

All I know is that I know nothing.

—Socrates

We've all been brought up to value answers and fear questions. We were rewarded for right answers at school and we are rewarded for bright ideas at work. No wonder so many people look for reasons to avoid doing research, especially qualitative research. Anxiety around looking less knowledgeable runs deep. At least quant stuff has the comforting familiarity of standardized testing. Maintaining a research mindset means realizing that bias is rampant, certainty is an illusion, and any answer has a short shelf life. A good question is far more valuable in the long run. And you can't ask good questions—meaning you can't learn—until you admit that you don't have the answers.

---

[6]Digital Services Georgia https://digitalservices.georgia.gov/
accessibility-case-study

2. Ask first, prototype later.

If we only test bottle openers, we may never realize customers prefer screw-top bottles.

—Victor Lombardi, Why We Fail

So, of course there is a rush to prototype and test the prototype. A prototype is an answer, and it's tangible, even if it's simply a sketch on paper. This is comfortable, much more comfortable than just asking questions, even if it is tantamount to setting a large pile of money on fire. To anyone concerned about demonstrating their value by making fast, visible progress, simply asking questions feels as productive as a raccoon washing cotton candy.

The danger in prototyping too soon is investing resources in answering a question no one asked and ignoring the opportunity cost. Testing a prototype can help you refine an idea that is already good, not tell you whether you're solving the right problem. And it's easy to mistake the polish of a prototype for the quality of the idea (cough Juicero cough). FWIW, it's also easy to mistake the gloss of a research report for the value of the insights.

Instead of saving and defending weak ideas, asking the right questions helps you identify and eradicate bad ideas faster. You just have to be strong enough to embrace being wrong.

3. Know your goal.

Asking questions is a waste of time unless you know your reason for doing so in advance. And you have to publicly swear that your reason is not "to be proven right."

That is everyone's secret goal. See number 1.

Often, in the enthusiasm to embrace research, teams will start talking to customers without a clear, shared goal. And then afterward, they feel like they spent precious time with no idea how to apply what they learned, hence nothing to show for it. This leads to statements like, "We tried doing research last year and it was a waste of time," and, thus, a return to the comfort of building and testing. Or they walk away with different interpretations of what they heard, which leads to more arguments about who was proven right.

In large organizations, the unspoken goal is sometimes "demonstrate a commitment to research while allowing our product leaders to do what they want." This might sound cynical, but I've talked to many skilled practitioners in well-funded research departments who generate magnificent reports that have zero impact on decision-making. Acknowledging this happens is the first step to stopping it.

It is perfectly fine and a great place to start for your goal to be "We need to level-set and quickly understand the perspective of people who aren't us." Just don't tack on other goals after the fact.

Only after you have a goal will you know what you need to know. And you have to know your question before you can choose how to answer it.

4. Agree on the big questions.

> *At its core, all business is about making bets on human behavior.*
>
> —The Power of "Thick" Data, WSJ

The quality of your question determines the utility of the results. Asking the wrong question is the same as prototyping a solution to the wrong problem. They will both give you something other than what you need. Start with your high-priority questions. These come from the assumptions or areas of ignorance that carry the most risk if you're wrong.

The big research question is what you want to know, not what you ask in an interview. In fact, asking your research question directly is often the worst way to learn anything. People often don't know or are unwilling to admit to their true behaviors, but everyone is really good at making up answers.

Design research gets conflated with user research all the time. Talking to representative users is just one of many ways of answering high-priority research questions. Not everything you need to know is about users.

Often the most critical question is a variation of "Based on evidence, what do we really know about our customers/competition/internal capabilities?" This can be a particularly terrifying one to approach in total honesty, but you should be able to answer it within the hour.

5. There is always enough time and money.

When research is defined as a type of work outside of design, it's easy to define gathering evidence as something extra and find reasons not to do it.

Often, teams have to ask permission of someone with authority in order to do work that is categorized as research. Asking questions is inherently threatening to authority. If you've ever worked with a leader who was resistant to doing qualitative research as part of a million-dollar project, ask yourself whether they would skip doing their own research before buying a $50,000 car. Stated objections are often cover for a fear of being undermined or proven wrong or not looking productive in the right way.

If you are clear and candid about your goals and high-priority questions, you can learn something useful within whatever time and budget is available to you. Find studies online. Go outside during lunch and observe people. Usability tests someone else's product. Get creative.

Just avoid doing surveys.

6. Don't expect data to change minds.

> *It is difficult to get a man to understand something, when his salary depends on his not understanding it.*
>
> —Upton Sinclair

This is often a hard one for highly trained, specialist researchers to embrace, even though research has demonstrated it to be true. If you are used to working with a community of peers who value a certain kind of data, you may be ill-equipped to convince people who reject it out of hand. And it can feel insulting to one's professional competence that the data is not enough.

The whole point of gathering evidence is to make evidence-based decisions. If that evidence undermines or contradicts the ideas of beliefs of the person with authority to make decisions, they will find reasons to reject it or ignore it. This is also at the heart of why qualitative researchers have a hard time in some engineering-driven organizations. People who are comfortable and competent with numbers want answers in numbers, even if the question demands something more descriptive.

So you have to turn ethnography inward and learn how your peers and leaders make decisions before you try to use data to influence those decisions.

7. Embrace messy imperfection.

> *We're fickle, stupid beings with poor memories and a great gift for self destruction.*

> —Suzanne Collins, Mockingjay

Human lives are messy. If people didn't have problems, there would be no need for products and services to solve them and we wouldn't have jobs. Figuring out the best way to solve problems for people requires some time out in the real, messy world and letting go of a certain amount of control. While an ethical, sufficiently rigorous approach is necessary, there is no qualitative clean room. A clear goal and a good question can withstand all sorts of unpredictable conditions.

The desire for tidy, comfortable activities that look and feel like expertise made visible leads to the inappropriate use of focus groups, usability labs, eye-tracking, surveys, and glossy reports when something much less formal would be much more effective.

Incorporating evidence into design decisions is itself a learning process. You will never find the right answer and be done. If the process is working, you will continue to make decisions with increasing levels of confidence.

8. Commit to collaboration.

Everyone working on the same thing needs to be operating in the same shared reality. The people making decisions about the product need to be the best informed. It doesn't matter how good the knowledge is if it's only in one person's head (unless you are in London and that person is your cab driver).

Research without collaboration means that one group of people is learning and creating reports for another group to acknowledge and ignore. Knowledge leaks out of even the most well-meaning teams working like this. Collaboration without evidence means everyone has tacitly agreed whose personal preferences win. Neither of these is the most productive approach.

Directly involving the people creating the product in asking and answering the questions is the most productive approach. Plus, it's fun. And there are several ways to accomplish this depending on the organization.

The whole point of asking questions is to establish a shared framework for making decisions so that you can make better decisions faster. It changes lives.

9. Find your bias buddies.

We can be blind to the obvious, and we are also blind to our blindness.

—Daniel Kahneman, Thinking Fast and Slow

So, you did the work and you found some answers. Now you need to decide what they mean. When it comes to interpreting the results of research, collaboration becomes particularly critical. Everyone with a human brain is burdened by human biases. And there is no way to sense one's own. We all see what best fits our existing beliefs. So, we have to refer to an external standard (including the pre-established goals and questions) and work together to check each other.

This has nothing to do with how smart or how well-informed you are. Once you accept this, and as long as you work in a team that evinces psychological safety and mutual respect, it can be a fun game to identify biases and call them out.

The Wikipedia page has a nice list, along with the Cognitive Bias Codex to print and post on your wall.

Maybe, just call it design done right.

In sum, what we're talking about when we're talking about design research is really doing evidence-based design. Creation, criticism, and inquiry are all integral parts of the design process. Separating them leads to optimizing for the wrong things out of ignorance, ego, or fear.

Design is an exchange of value. You have to ask what people really need and value and what business value you expect to get in return, before putting anything at all into the world.

It doesn't matter what questions you ask or how you find the answers, as long as you are ethical in your approach, honest about what you know, and apply yourself toward a worthwhile goal. There is no one right way and no one right answer. Enjoy the uncertainty! It never ends.[7]

Conclusion

Research is a valuable piece of the equation of making a product that will be usable. Research can often take a lot of time to conduct and many in the field have advanced degrees in the area of analysis and research. When possible, hire a professional researcher; it can help in cases of very large and complex projects or if your team does not have the bandwidth to conduct research. When it comes to making your product more accessible

---

[7]Nine rules of design research https://muledesign.com/2018/02/
the-9-rules-of-design-research

and inclusive, you will want to take the time and plan things out properly. Here are some tips for planning your research:

- Identifying stakeholders

- Proper documentation

- Defining your problem

- Research

- User research

- User journey

- Personas with disabilities

- Evaluation criteria

CHAPTER 7

Assistive Technologies

For people without disabilities, technology makes things easier. For people with disabilities, technology makes things possible.

—IBM Training Manual 1991

Do you wear glasses or contacts? You may not think about those things as assistive technology but in many ways they are. They make things more accessible to you. Creating accessible experiences, often times, can open our eyes to things that we didn't know existed with the technology we use on a daily basis. The beauty of technology is that it can be made for all of us. Accessibility often ends up benefitting all of us and allows for ease of use with our products.

In this chapter, we'll start with a brief overview of assistive technologies and then look at several assistive technologies and how they assist people with disabilities and their experiences. More resources can be found in the appendix.

© Regine M. Gilbert 2019
R. M. Gilbert, *Inclusive Design for a Digital World*,
https://doi.org/10.1007/978-1-4842-5016-7_7

Who, What, Where, When, Why, and How

In application of the W5H (who, what, where, when, why, and how), assistive technologies is the what. As creators, having knowledge of the different types of assistive technologies one might use, can help you understand how people might use your products or services.

When you think about the individuals who will use your product, you can ask yourself the following questions: Are they accessing your product via Web, mobile, or a voice assistant? What are they using to access your product?

It's good to take a look out there and see what is happening. I Googled "Assistive Technologies for tech", and got the results shown in Figure 7-1.

Figure 7-1. *Google search of Assistive Technology for tech*

What Is Assistive Technology?

Assistive technology (AT) is a general term that includes assistive, adaptive, and rehabilitative devices for people with disabilities, including the process used in selecting, locating, and using them. Assistive technology promotes greater independence by enabling people to perform tasks that they were formerly unable to accomplish, or had great difficulty accomplishing, by providing enhancements to, or changing methods of interacting with, the technology needed to accomplish such tasks. Assistive technology products are designed to provide additional accessibility to individuals who have physical or cognitive difficulties, impairments, and disabilities. There are so many instances where, through minor modifications, you can make a mainstream product accessible. Nevertheless, there are also situations where your only option is assistive technology.

Adaptive Technology vs. Assistive Technology

The term adaptive technology is often used as the synonym for assistive technology; however, they are different terms. Assistive technology refers to "any item, piece of equipment, or product system, whether acquired commercially, modified, or customized, that is used to increase, maintain, or improve functional capabilities of individuals with disabilities," while adaptive technology covers items that are specifically designed for persons with disabilities and would seldom be used by nondisabled persons.

If you have a disability or injury, you may use a number of assistive devices or rehabilitation equipment to aid you in and around the home. Assistive devices are tools, products, or types of equipment that help you perform tasks and activities if you have a disability or injury or are a senior. Assistive devices may help you move around, see, communicate, eat, or get dressed/undressed.

Assistive devices for mobility/ambulation can also be referred to as ambulatory aids. Ambulatory aids (e.g., canes, crutches, walkers) are used to provide an extension of the upper extremities to help transmit body weight and provide support for the user.

Assistive devices can help you improve your quality of life and maintain your sense of independence.

Well-designed high-quality assistive devices, or daily living aids, that support independent living for the disabled, seniors, or those with a medical condition or injury should make life easier and safer for the aged and disabled.

AT promotes greater independence by enabling people to perform tasks that they were formerly unable to accomplish, or had great difficulty accomplishing, by providing enhancements to or changed methods of interacting with the technology needed to accomplish such tasks.

An assistive device could be a wheelchair, reacher, or a disability product that allows you to use a computer. If you experience difficulties performing certain tasks, it is possible that an assistive device can help you overcome your problems.

Other disability aids include

- Advanced technology walking products to aid people with disabilities, such as paraplegia or cerebral palsy, who would not at all be able to walk or stand (exoskeletons)

- Standing products to support people with disabilities in the standing position while maintaining/improving their health (standing frame, standing wheelchair, active stander)

- Seating products that assist people to sit comfortably and safely (seating systems, cushions, therapeutic seats)

- Walking products to aid people with disabilities who are able to walk or stand with assistance (canes, crutches, walkers, gait trainers)

- Wheeled mobility products that enable people with reduced mobility to move freely indoors and outdoors (e.g., wheelchairs and scooters)

Certain devices, such as eyeglasses and hearing aids, obviously require an expert's assessment, but many assistive devices for the enhancement of daily life such as wheelchairs, walkers, bath seats, and grab bars are easily obtainable in general and specialty stores including online disability product web sites.

You will also find pharmacy personnel are usually quite happy to provide information on a variety of other assistive products like magnifying glasses, bath seats, joint support bandages, pill organizers, canes, etc.

Specialty computer stores often carry items like screen reading software that include screen enlargement features for persons with vision impairments. Voice recognition systems, modified keyboards, and computer mice are also available for people with mobility and dexterity limitations.

When selecting assistive technology products for computers, it is crucial to find the right products that are compatible with the computer operating system and programs on the particular computer you will be using.

Screen Readers

Screen readers are software that can live within a device such as computers and mobile devices. Figure 7-2 shows how a user interacts with a screen reader. Notice that first the screen reader identifies text or graphics, then the screen reader navigates the page, then screen readers read text or graphics, then the keyboard or voice is used to navigate the web page, and finally text or graphics are read back to the user as speech or braille.

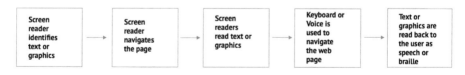

Figure 7-2. *User flow of screen reader*

The following are some example of the types of software available:

- Screen readers: Software used by blind or visually impaired people to read the content of the computer screen. Examples include JAWS for Windows, or NVDA. Figure 7-3 shows JAWS (Job Access With Speech) screen reader software, the world's most popular screen reader, developed for computer users whose vision loss prevents them from seeing screen content or navigating with a mouse.[1]

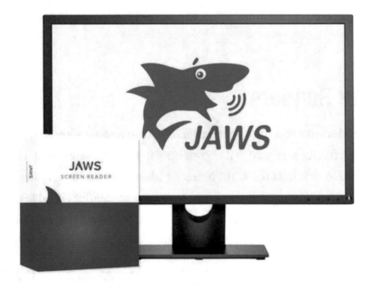

Figure 7-3. *JAWS screen reader software*

- Screen magnification software: Allow users to control the size of text and or graphics on the screen. Unlike using a zoom feature, these applications allow the user to have the ability to see the enlarged text in relation

---

[1]Freedom Scientific JAWS Logo www.freedomscientific.com/products/software/jaws/

to the rest of the screen. This is done by emulating a handheld magnifier over the screen. The American Federation for the blind has a few recommendations for free alternatives.[2] Figure 7-4 shows a screen magnifier called Dragnifier.

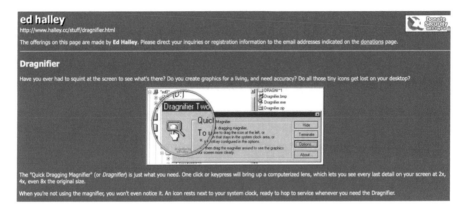

Figure 7-4. *Ed Halley's screen magnifier "Dragnifier"*

- Zoom-in browsers can help those with vision impairments see text and images on the screen. Figure 7-5 shows an Amazon home page magnified 400% on Chrome.

---

[2]A review of Freeware and Shareware screen magnification software for Windows www.afb.org/aw/14/4/15707

Figure 7-5. *Image of Amazon home page magnified at 400%*

- Text readers: Software used by people with various forms of learning disabilities that affect their ability to read text. This software will read text with a synthesized voice and may have a highlighter to emphasize the word being spoken. These applications do not read things such as menus or types of elements—they only read the text. Figure 7-6 shows one of the more popular text readers: Natural Readers.

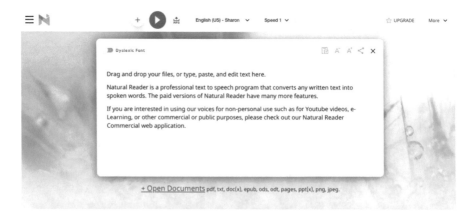

Figure 7-6. *Natural Readers instructions for their text reader* www.naturalreaders.com/online/

- Speech input software: Provides people with difficulty in typing an alternate way to type text and also control the computer. Users can give the system some limited commands to perform mouse actions. Users can tell the system to click a link or a button or use a menu item. Please note both Windows and Mac have some speech recognition utilities, but they cannot be used to browse the Web. Figure 7-7 shows Apple's voice-over feature, which is available for Apple devices.

Figure 7-7. *Voice-over pop-up on Apple computer*

- Alternative input devices: Some users may not be able to use a mouse or keyboard to work on a computer. These people can use various forms of devices, such as

  - Head pointers: A stick or object mounted directly on the user's head that can be used to push keys on the keyboard. This device is used by individuals who have no use of their hands. Figure 7-8 shows a head pointer and stylus.

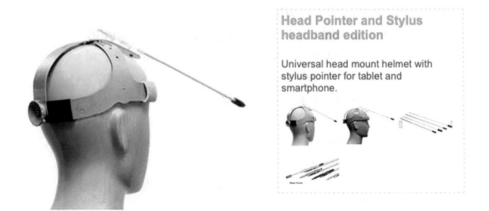

Figure 7-8. *Head pointer and stylus headband edition* `www.`
`unitedspinal.org/disability-products-services/mundstab-`
`mouthstick---mouth-head-sticks/`

- Motion tracking or eye tracking: This can include
  devices that watch a target or even the eyes of the user
  to interpret where the user wants to place the mouse
  pointer and moves it for the user. Figure 7-9 shows an
  eye with the camera and the gaze of the user's eyes.

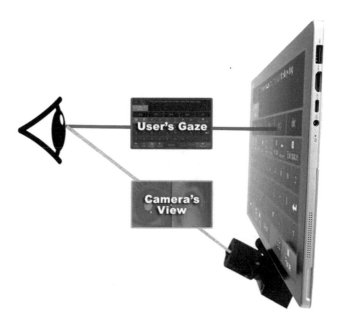

Figure 7-9. *Eyegaze eye-driven tablet communication system*
`https://eyegaze.com/products/eyegaze-edge/`

- Single switch entry devices: These kinds of devices
  can be used with other alternative input devices or by
  themselves. These are typically used with on-screen
  keyboards. The on-screen keyboard has a cursor move
  across the keys, and when the key the user wants is
  in focus, the user will click the switch. This can also
  work on a web page: the cursor can move through
  the web page, and if the user wants a to click a link or
  button when that link or button is in focus, the user
  can activate the switch. Figure 7-10 shows a switch
  controller in yellow and white.

Figure 7-10. *Switch controller* www.boundlessat.com/Switches

Some assistive technologies are built into devices and some are stand-alone technologies that work along with web browsers.

Web browsers have built in accessibility that will work with assistive technologies. In the next section, we will look at some of the most used web browsers and the accessibility features they have available.

Web Browsers

In 2019, the top browsers in the United States for searching the Web are[3]

- Mozilla Firefox

- Google Chrome

- Opera

- Microsoft Edge

- Microsoft Internet Explorer

If you do not currently use the accessibility features, you may not know what is available for people with disabilities. For each browser, there are

---

[3]Top five web browsers www.techradar.com/news/the-best-web-browser

different accessibility features, which are available for people's individual needs. Let's take a look at some of Mozilla's accessibility features.

Mozilla is widely used and is the number one browser in the United States. It has a lot to offer! Firefox includes many features to make the browser and web content accessible to all users including those who have low vision, no vision, or limited ability to use a keyboard or mouse.[4]

This section will cover keyboard use, mouse shortcuts, using high-contrast theme, controlling web content, and compatibility with assistive technologies.

Looking these over also gives you an opportunity to try these accessibility features on your own.

Keyboards

There are folks who may only use a keyboard to navigate web pages. Understanding the way different browsers work with keyboard navigation can be helpful when creating experiences. Let's take a look at Firefox.

Using a Keyboard to Navigate Within Web Pages

In your Firefox Preferences in the General panel, the *Browsing* section includes the setting **Always use the cursor keys to navigate within webpages** which allows you to move through web content as if you were inside a read-only editor. You can use the keyboard to select web content and copy it to the clipboard.

You can press F7 at any time to turn this feature on or off. When you press F7, Firefox will ask if you really want to turn on this feature. You can disable this prompt by selecting **Do not show this dialog again**.

---

[4]Accessibility features in Firefox—make Firefox and web content work for all users
`https://support.mozilla.org/en-US/kb/accessibility-features-firefox-make-firefox-and-we`

Searching for Text When You Start to Type

In your Firefox Preferences in the General panel, the *Browsing* section includes the setting **Search for text when you start typing**. This allows you to quickly navigate to text or hyperlinks in a web page. This feature has two modes. Press / and start typing to search all text on the current page, or press ' before your string to search hyperlinks only. Firefox will highlight matching text or hyperlinks as you type.

The following keyboard shortcuts control this feature:

- Type more characters to narrow your search. Firefox will highlight the next matching hyperlink or text or alert you that nothing matched.

- Press command+G or F3 to find the next occurrence of your current search string.

- Press command+Shift+G or Shift+F3 to find the previous occurrence of your current search string.

- Press Backspace to undo the last character you typed. Firefox will back up to the previously highlighted text.

- Press Esc to cancel a search. You can also cancel a search by changing focus or simply waiting for the timeout.

HTML Access Keys

On some web pages, keyboard shortcuts are assigned to different elements on the page. To move the cursor directly to one of these elements, press Ctrl + option+*AccessKey*.

Which key *AccessKey* is depends on the web site. It is determined by the web site author, not Firefox.

Zoom, Fonts, and Colors

You can zoom in and out of web pages including images with the following keyboard shortcuts:

- Press command++ to display the web page one size larger.

- Press command+- to display the web page one size smaller.

- Press command+0 (zero) to display the web page at its normal size.

You can choose to change the text size only using the *Text Zoom* feature:

1. On the menu bar, click the View menu, and then go to Zoom.

2. Select Zoom Text Only, which will make the controls only apply to text, not images.

The following keyboard shortcuts control text size when Text Zoom is selected:

- Press command++ to increase the text size.

- Press command+- to decrease the text size.

- Press command+0 (zero) to reset the text size to the web page's default size.

Note that some web pages may display incorrectly if you increase or decrease the text size.

Other accessibility features on Mozilla Firefox include

- Setting fonts and colors

- Setting a minimum font size

- Overriding page fonts

- Overriding page colors

- Blocking pop-up windows

- Restricting JavaScript behavior

Try This

- Use the zoom feature (go up to 400%) on your browser and see if you can navigate the page.

The other browsers like Mozilla have accessibility features built in that can be used with assistive technologies. The full list of links to resources for these features can be found in the appendix.

Mobile

We live in an Android and iOS world when it comes to our devices. Both sets of devices have accessibility built into them. Table 7-1 lists the accessibility features for the latest phones side by side.

Table 7-1. *Mobile phone accessibility features*

Features	iOS Accessibility Features for Mobile	Android Accessibility Features for Mobile
Modification of Text	X	X
Screen Magnification	X	X
Digital Pay Systems	X	X
Screen Readers	X	X
Color Inversion	X	X

When it comes to features, both Android and iOS measure almost equally. However, when it comes to ease of use, many have said that iOS is a lot easier to use. Ultimately, what is best for you is the best.

In recent years, we have seen an emergence in Voice User Interfaces (VUI). Alexa, Google, and Cortana have been weaved into our lives, and we now consider the use of voice assistants in our home the new normal.

Having both Google Home and Alexa has provided us with abilities to get the weather, make phone calls, and experience entertainment. For people with disabilities, voice assistants have brought about new opportunities for saving time and assisting when needed.

Voice Assistants

Let's take a look at how voice assistants are changing the lives of the disabled from the actual people who use them.

"It Saves Valuable Time"

Robin Christopherson, head of digital inclusion at *AbilityNet*, makes a great case for AI for accessibility by explaining how the disabled community is benefiting the most from the escalating efforts of tech giants.

Being visually impaired himself, he found that virtual assistants such as Siri, Cortana, and Google Now already save him and other people with disabilities valuable time when getting things done.

No more battling with screen readers and "accessible web sites" for Christopherson. He adds, "What Siri can do in 5 seconds might take me 5 minutes, or sometimes 10!"[5]

---

[5]Voice assistants are changing how user with disabilities get things done
www.modev.com/blog/voice-assistants-are-changing-how-users-with-disabilities-get-things-done

It's amazing to see the difference these products created for entertainment purposes can actually help everyone get things more efficiently.

Table 7-2 lists some of the features for some of the popular voice assistants.

Table 7-2. *Voice assistant features*

	Alexa	Google Home	Cortana
Vision	Large text setting for App (not for iOS)	Screen reader for Nest display	Use of Narrator
Hearing	Pair Alexa with Bluetooth	Play alert sounds (visual indicators available)	Type what you want to do—see response
Mobility	Keyboard navigation	Media controls	Keyboard navigation
Speech	Customized Wake words	Change language	Talk to text

How gamers with disabilities helped design the new Xbox Adaptive Controller's elegantly accessible packaging Case Study

Think about the last time you had to open a package that was difficult to open. Todays electronics, including gaming systems can have challenging packaging. Twist ties that bedevil, thick plastic requiring scissors to break open, tape that gets wrapped around fingers, and those cursed strips known as zip ties; packaging can be annoying for any consumer. But for people with disabilities, it often creates yet another challenge in a world riddled with them, an unnecessary obstacle that leads to frustration and a delay getting to the object inside.

Recognizing that reality, Microsoft's Packaging Design team faced a unique challenge in creating a box for the new Xbox Adaptive Controller, designed to accommodate gamers with limited mobility. The box for the device, which will be available for $99.99 in September through the

Microsoft Store, needed to be as accessible as what was inside. It had to enable gamers with limited dexterity, who might be using just one hand or arm, to easily open the box and remove the controller. And it had to be as high-quality and aesthetically appealing as any other Xbox packaging.

It was the first time Microsoft had created packaging designed specifically for accessibility, and getting it right was critical.

"The product team was putting so much diligence into getting the controller right that to not have a package that was thoughtfully and mindfully designed for the end user would have felt like a real miss," said Kevin Marshall, creative director of Microsoft's Packaging Design Studio.

"With this product in particular, we felt a heightened responsibility. We wanted to create a package that was clearly designed with the end user in mind, and we wanted it to feel like it was just part of our ecosystem," he said. "We wanted it to be empowering, but we didn't want it to stand apart from any package we create."

Solomon Romney, a Microsoft Stores retail learning specialist in Salt Lake City, Utah, was among the gamers who tested the packaging as it was being developed. The extra attention to accessibility, he said, creates a positive experience from the start.

"It's great that we've created this controller for people to use, but if they can't even get it out of the box, we've sort of fallen on our face with this whole process. This makes such a huge difference in how someone gets our device out of the package," he said. "I still think about it and think, why isn't more packaging like this?"

Mark Weiser, the Microsoft designer who created the packaging, started by looking for examples of other accessible packaging. He found little that excited him, and even the accessible products Weiser looked at weren't often packaged in ways that made them easy to open. It benefits everybody to have a package that opens a lot faster, with less hassle.

Weiser worked closely with Xbox design researcher Scott Wang, who consulted with gamers and disability advocates as the Xbox Adaptive Controller was being developed. Their feedback helped shape many of the device's features, including the packaging. Weiser had already decided not to use twist ties, but the gamers Wang spoke with provided other key insights, including one main stipulation—no teeth. They told Wang about using their teeth to open everything from cereal boxes to beer bottles. If nothing else, they said, the box should not require teeth to open.

The gamers also said they'd prefer more simple steps to open the box than fewer but more complicated steps. Being able to access the controller from multiple points was also important. And the gamers identified a feature that became a key part of the package's design—loops that enable users to easily open the box and remove the controller. Weiser added a loop on the outside of the specially designed retail shipping box so users could easily remove the sealing tape. Another loop opens the interior box holding the controller, which has a hinged opening rather than a lid that could require two hands to remove.

Yet another loop is integrated into the quick-start guide sitting under the controller. A user who can't reach into the space under the controller and slide it out (another accessibility feature) can use the loop to remove it. And since the controller has grippy feet to hold it in place for gamers who might play on wheelchair trays or tables, the loop on the guide eliminates the possibility of the controller sticking to the paper tray under it. An additional loop on the paper encircling the controller cables makes them easy to remove.

Other accessibility features include folding the warranty and compliance guide on the long edge to minimize the amount of arm movement required and centering the controller in the box to provide greater stability.

The designs and materials used for the other components were also carefully considered. The retail box is made of a rigid paperboard that provides additional device protection and offers less resistance than other papers when opened. The pulp tray under the controller is open at the front for easy device removal, which required extra technical and design attention. Paper is the medium of choice for Microsoft packaging, as it's more environmentally friendly, and plastics are avoided unless absolutely necessary.

Since Weiser was creating the packaging as the controller was being developed, he needed to adapt the box as the device evolved. Even small changes to the controller required him to reevaluate how the box interacted with it—for example, ensuring that the two large buttons added to the top of the device wouldn't be clicked repeatedly if the box was jostled. The final packaging involved more than 100 iterations of its various components, Weiser said.

"It became an incredibly deep and broad scope of work," Marshall said. "That's part of the fun. That's part of our learning process. We learn by doing. We learn by building, and on this particular product, there was a lot to learn."

As he was developing the packaging, Weiser tested it with multiple Microsoft employees who have limited mobility. One of the employees, Weiser said, was doubtful he'd be able to open the box, given his usual difficulties with packaging. But to his surprise, it opened more easily than expected.

"It was really great to see him be excited about it," Weiser said.

Microsoft designers enlisted gamers with disabilities to test a variety of prototypes in order to make the packaging more accessible. The Microsoft team also tested the packaging with several gamers in the United States and the United Kingdom, including Mike Luckett, an avid gamer from Colorado who has limited mobility in his fingers from a spinal injury he sustained in a motorcycle accident. Luckett provided feedback on typical packaging pitfalls, from paper cuts caused by perforated or corrugated edges to the plastic covers some controllers come in, which he finds "incredibly frustrating" and difficult to open.

"I'm excited that Microsoft is taking the opportunity to try to understand individuals who have less ability to open a traditional package than able-bodied users," he said. "Having this easy-to-open packaging doesn't just benefit us in the disabled community. It benefits everybody to have a package that opens a lot faster, with less hassle, so you can game faster."

Romney was shown three prototypes of the packaging. Born without fingers on his left hand, he tested the models using that hand only. Based on Romney's feedback, the loops on the packaging were created in an oval shape to accommodate gamers who might not be able to navigate a smaller circular loop. Romney appreciated the loops and the overall ease and elegance of the packaging.

"The whole thing sort of blossoms open in this really beautiful, fluid way," he said. "The package just sort of opens and hands you the controller. What's wonderful about it is the effortlessness."

I think as a case study of inclusive design, the Xbox Adaptive Controller is going to make a brilliant example of how you do it and how you include your audience and design *with* a population, rather than *for* a population. Romney said the experience has made him think about packaging differently.

"We have customers in our store every single day who buy product. I look at our laptop boxes and how they have to be opened. How many steps, how much packaging, and how much of a barrier do each of those pieces become to someone with a mobility limitation?"

Romney thinks the Xbox Adaptive Controller packaging has the potential to set a new standard.

"I think it's going to change how we look at things in the industry, in terms of how we make boxes. And I think it has to," he said. "I think as a case study of inclusive design, the Xbox Adaptive Controller is going to make a brilliant example of how you do it, and how you include your audience and design *with* a population, rather than *for* a population."

For Marshall and Weiser, the packaging project was challenging, time-consuming—and ultimately rewarding.

"It was a really powerful experience," Marshall said. "I don't think you realize, until you're required to think differently, what you take for granted. As a designer, when you see things through a completely different lens, it's paradigm-shifting."

142

Said Weiser: "We put in a lot of extra time on it, but it was a pleasure to be able to work on this type of project. It's great that we're focused on this as a company."

Discussions are underway about how Microsoft might use the learnings from the Xbox Adaptive Controller packaging. Marshall hopes the deceptively simple-looking box can serve as a springboard for future efforts.

"It's certainly changing how we're looking at packaging. We're excited about moving forward from this point with a new lens and looking at what we can do," he said.

"We're really excited to take this journey on."[6]

The Future of Assistive Technology

This is a very exciting time for new developments in assistive technology. Not only are existing AT programs regularly updated, but new and previously unseen technology is en route to improve accessibility for persons with disabilities. With the advent of e-book readers like Kindle, Sony E-reader, and recently the Nook released by Barnes and Noble, there could be another wave of new methods for people with learning disabilities and other conditions to access e-books and books. While not all of the devices have text-to-speech capability, some of them do, and if it proves useful, other producers of e-book readers will probably follow suit and adopt that utility in the near future.

---

[6]"How gamers with disabilities helped design the new xbox adaptive controller" nhttps://news.microsoft.com/features/how-gamers-with-disabilities-helped-design-the-new-xbox-adaptive-controllers-elegantly-accessible-packaging/

By current estimates, more than 4,000 assistive technologies have been designed for the disabled and seniors. These devices include everything from wheelchairs to a wide assortment of high-tech tools, and many companies today are turning their research and development to assistive technologies.[7]

Conclusion

There is so much to be explored and yet to be created when it comes to assistive technologies and the devices we use today. In Chapter 10, we will discuss emerging technologies related to accessibility. Having an understanding of the types of technologies associated with accessibility helps us move forward with being able to figure out the best way to build our products. In the next chapter, we will look at integrating accessibility into our design and development systems.

Every goal is possible from here. We live in a technologically advanced world that has provided us with tools and the skills to build more accessible products so that we can use them today and as our older selves when things that once worked one way have gone to a different way of working.

---

[7]Assistive Technologies www.disabled-world.com/assistivedevices/

CHAPTER 8

Planning and Implementing Inclusive Designs

Accessibility must be part of every aspect of business, part of the minimally viable product, a core part of how we approach the launch and growth of our platforms.

—David Peter

Implementing accessibility/inclusivity and making changes to workflow can come with many opportunities. Change does not often come easily. Making swift changes can cause friction between teams and individuals. Implementing change needs to be approached with understanding for what each team will need to address. Laying out how people can participate in the process is helpful. Whether you are a designer or developer, the tips in this chapter will guide you in these areas.

- Creating a culture of inclusivity/accessibility
- When to begin incorporating inclusive design in the process
- Accessible documentation

© Regine M. Gilbert 2019
R. M. Gilbert, *Inclusive Design for a Digital World*,
https://doi.org/10.1007/978-1-4842-5016-7_8

Creating a Culture of Inclusivity/ Accessibility

Creating a culture of accessibility is not the job of a single person; it takes a village to make accessible products. Having leadership buy-in is absolutely key to having accessibility instituted into a team. But what if you don't have buy-in?

When leadership does not support incorporating accessibility in the design and development of digital products, it can make it difficult to get things done. If you're reading this book, you have some interest in learning more about accessibility. If you are the only one knowing about it, learning the benefits accessibility provides for your business can be helpful when trying to get others to look at things differently.

Planting seeds is one way to include something new into the workflow. What one can do is plant the seed of why accessibility and inclusivity are important. This means making small recommendations or changes to incorporate accessibility in the workflow or educating others on what is means to learning, and implementation accessibility is an ongoing process. Speaking of the benefits can offer people a new perspective. The benefits of accessibility (Figure 8-1) can not only have an impact on your business, they can have a positive impact for your customers as well. The following sections explain how. Benefits of accessibility include increasing your audience and potential of financial benefits from a wider audience.

Figure 8-1. *Benefits of accessibility*

Avoiding Discrimination and Legal Complaints

As the Internet and other digital technologies become increasingly prevalent in daily life, it's not hard to argue that web accessibility is a civil right for people with disabilities. The Americans with Disabilities Act (ADA) requires that people with disabilities can enjoy equal access to public services and "places of public accommodation" such as restaurants, movie theaters, and schools.

While the ADA does not explicitly address the question of web accessibility yet, the legislation is broad enough that it is interpreted to extend into the digital sphere as well. In a number of legal cases, the US Department of Justice has concluded that the lack of accessibility for web sites may be a violation of the ADA.

The number of web accessibility lawsuits is growing rapidly. In 2018, there were 2,258 web accessibility lawsuits filed in the United States, nearly tripling from the 814 lawsuits in 2017. A number of recent high-profile cases, such as a lawsuit against the web site of the singer Beyoncé, have also increased visibility and awareness.

Businesses that want to avoid claims of discrimination and legal action should work to implement web accessibility standards such as the Web Content Accessibility Guidelines (WCAG). They can also obtain a Letter of Reasonable Accessibility testifying that their web site has been audited and has made reasonable accommodations for people with disabilities.

Reaching a Wider Audience

Disabilities come in many different forms, including hearing disabilities, visual disabilities, motor disabilities, and cognitive disabilities. The US Centers for Disease Control and Prevention (CDC) estimate that one in four US adults is living with a disability.

Businesses and organizations should therefore ignore this segment of the population at their own peril.

Improving your web site's accessibility is simply good business sense. Although it's not possible to design a web site that's accessible to everyone on the planet, a few common-sense modifications can go a long way toward helping people with disabilities use your site. What's more, features such as transcripts and closed captions, support for mobile devices, and a clear, simple site design will be beneficial for all users, not simply those who require them due to a disability.

Building Positive PR

In this era of digital activism, many consumers want to support companies that share their beliefs, ideals, and values. According to a recent survey by Accenture Strategy, 62% of consumers prefer to make purchases from a brand that is willing to take a stand on issues that matter. What's more, 47% are willing to walk away if they are disappointed with a company's words or actions, and 17% will not return.

Web accessibility is an important cause for people with disabilities, their loved ones, and disability rights advocates. By taking a stand on web accessibility, you'll be building the foundation of a positive brand image for your organization. People with disabilities who have positive interactions with your business are more likely to recommend you to their family, friends, acquaintances, and social media connections.

One way to start generating positive PR is to write an accessibility statement for your web site. This document states your commitment to web accessibility and describes the steps that you have taken to accommodate people with disabilities, such as complying with web accessibility frameworks like WCAG.

Improving SEO

Creating an accessible web site does more than make your site more usable—it also makes your site more likely to be found by improving search engine optimization (SEO).

The goal of SEO is to drive more traffic to your content by improving your web site's ranking in search engines such as Google. While the exact details of how pages are ranked in Google are never fully revealed, there are some SEO best practices that nearly all digital marketers can agree on.

In many cases, the goals of web accessibility and SEO are aligned. Building web sites with cleaner interfaces and easier navigation helps people with disabilities, but it also improves your bounce rate (the percentage of visitors who leave your web site after only one-page visit).

Increasing Usability

Just as web accessibility and SEO are linked, so too are web accessibility and usability. The goal of accessibility is to make products, services, and environments more usable by people with disabilities. In this light, accessibility can be seen as a sub-case or overlapping concept of usability, which aims to improve a product or service's ease of use and user experience.

For example, web accessibility standards such as WCAG require web sites to be entirely usable and navigable with only the keyboard (i.e., without the use of a mouse). Of course, this benefits people who may have challenges operating a standard computer mouse.

However, making your web site navigable with a keyboard also benefits your broader user base. Fulfilling this requirement implies that the navigational elements of your web site are well-organized in a strict hierarchy, which will help all users more easily locate the content they need.

Other web accessibility recommendations will also improve the general usability of your site. For example, alternative text for images and objects on your web site can help people with slow Internet connections understand the purpose of the content before it loads. Glossaries with definitions of acronyms, rare words, and technical terms are useful for some people with cognitive disabilities, some people who speak English as a second language, and everyone at different times.

Writing Higher-Quality Code

As one final advantage for your developers and designers, web sites that are created with accessibility in mind tend to have a higher-quality code base. For example, accessibility testing tools such as the a11y testing platform can also identify errors that create general problems with usability.

Writing cleaner code has a variety of benefits for your web site, including better user interfaces, fewer bugs, and faster loading times (which will also improve your SEO ranking as a result). In this light, accessibility should be seen as an investment in your code base and the future of your business.[1]

Accessibility Tidbits

Types of impairments that affect how people use your digital product

- Visual
- Auditory
- Cognitive
- Mobility

---

[1]Benefits of web accessibility `www.boia.org/blog/6-unexpected-benefits-of-web-accessibility`

Accessibility benefits everyone:

- People not fluent in English
- People who are unable to use a keyboard or mouse
- People with temporary disabilities due to accident and illness
- Older people and new users

Three reasons to make your digital product accessible

1. Increase your audience and customer base
2. May provide significant financial benefits
3. The better thing to do morally and legally

Did you know globally, people with a disability have a combined annual disposable income of $996 billion? Your content needs to be accessible to everyone.[2]

Depending on the digital product you are working on, you may have some internal data that you can use to speak of additional benefits of accessibility. By speaking and sharing the benefits to the overall business, it is more likely that you will get buy-in. It may take some time, and it is definitely worth the effort.

Once they become open to the idea of accessibility, see about bringing in people with disabilities to work on your team. Organizations like The Disabled List is a disability-led, self-advocacy organization that is creating the opportunities in design that we always wanted. The Disabled List is a curated list of creative disabled people who are available to consult. WITH, the first program of the Disabled List, is a fellowship that partners disabled creatives with design studios and branding agencies.[3] Working with disabled partners have been proven to create products that are more accessible.

---

[2]Source: US Census, US Labor of Statistics, Statistics Canada, Eurostat, FQA—in USD
[3]Disabled List www.disabledlist.org

If there is not an accessibility professional on the team, it's recommended to bring in accessibility experts to audit your product and let you know where your gaps are with accessibility.

Incorporating Accessibility into Design Systems

If you work in an environment that is interested in incorporating accessibility into your daily workflows, there are ways to incorporate it into designs before anything is coded. Having a design system that includes accessibility can help clear up many questions that usually occur after a product is built. Design systems can benefit teams by including the following:

- Ensure that the team has an understanding of accessibility in relation to your product (the team or a professional can put together guidelines specific to your product).

- Include accessibility into user stories, wireframes, and requirements.

- Make it clear that each team is responsible for accessibility and inform them of what their responsibilities are (copy, visual designers, developers, etc.).

- Document navigation clearly.

- Guidance of use of colors, forms, and focus of navigation.

- Maintaining documentation for reference when new members come onto a team.

There is no one-size-fits-all option for design systems; you have to work within your teams and determine what is the best solution for who you work with. Overall, design systems can help teams understand and use the right type of tools for the job of making things more accessible and in return getting more people to use the product. There is no one-size-fits-all option for design systems, you have to work within your teams and determine what is the best solution for who you work with.

Implementing Accessibility

After you have found a way to include accessibility, you then have to implement it. Where do you begin?

- Establish responsibilities.

- Conduct an initial audit.

- Develop an organizational policy.

- Select software for evaluating and repairing web accessibility.

- Provide training.

- Promote accessibility throughout the organization.

- Monitor accessibility.[4]

Figure 8-2 shows what an organization structure of an accessible team might look like.

---

[4]Implementation plan for web accessibility www.w3.org/WAI/impl/resp

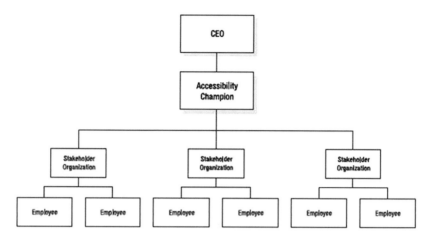

Figure 8-2. *Accessibility Organization Structure - Jim Thatcher*

Conclusion

When you are able to include accessibility and plan for it, it does not guarantee success, but your chances for getting more people to use your product are a lot higher. If you do not have the expertise in-house, then it's best to bring in an expert in accessibility to help get your teams do the work they need to do. Resources for accessibility experts are in the appendix. After you have implemented and executed accessibility, you will need to think about usability testing. We will cover this in the next chapter.

CHAPTER 9

Usability Testing

In this chapter, we'll focus on testing products with people with disabilities. We'll start by reviewing what makes a good product and see how to recruit people with disabilities. We'll then examine usability testing best practices. Most of this will be covered in a BBC iPlayer Case Study.

Knowing Your Product Is Good Enough

> *One of the biggest obstacles is the attitude that accessibility is charity. "Oh, I'll deal with it later because we don't have time." Disability tech is an investment in you. All of our bodies change. Design it with access in mind.*
>
> —Haben Girma

From my experience working in technology for many years, there has been a repeated pattern of individuals and organizations not testing their products and more particularly not testing products for or with people with disabilities. Testing your product before you launch can help the product's success. There will be times that you will have more questions than answers. To get to those answers, testing will help.

Let me say first that there is a difference between user testing and usability testing. The user is the person who will be using your product or service, and if you are running user testing, you are testing the persons (user needs) who will use your product or service.

© Regine M. Gilbert 2019
R. M. Gilbert, *Inclusive Design for a Digital World*,
https://doi.org/10.1007/978-1-4842-5016-7_9

Usability refers to the actual functionality of your product or service. You can sometimes combine both types of testing; however, it is best to keep them separate because the typical goal of creating a product is to see if someone can use it, and the surefire way to see that is through people experiencing your product or service. Figure 9-1 shows user testing vs. usability testing. When working on a product or service, think about what do your users need? Have you incorporated accessibility into the functionality of your product? Is your product or service usable? Have you tested it outside of your organization?

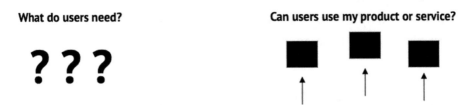

Figure 9-1. *User testing: What do users need? Usability testing: Can users use my product or service?*

Testing products with people with disabilities can increase the number of people who use your products and ensure that you are making more inclusive experiences overall. The barriers that exist in technology are not from the people, but from the creators of the technology. With the wide range of disabilities out there, it can feel overwhelming to know how and what to test for. There is some education involved with understanding how people with disabilities will use your products and what types of assistive technologies they may use.

Take the time to get familiar with how people with disabilities may use your product or service. It is best to observe the experts in assistive technologies, the ones who use the products on a daily basis. If you are not able to see people in person, there are great resources online. Resources for learning more are available in the appendix.

Think of the functionality of your product or service. You may think, how can I test for everything? The truth is that you cannot test for everything; however, you can look at the four areas (vision, hearing, cognition, and mobility) and think of the functionality of your product or service and see if you are fitting the needs of people with disabilities.

Questions you will want to ask before usability testing include

- What will you test for?

- What is your product trying to achieve?

- How much time do you have?

- How much money do you have?

- How many resources are available for testing?

- Will you need special equipment or devices?

- What will your users need to do?

    - And if they have different ways of accessing your products, have you given them a way to do so?

Usability answers the question, "Can the user accomplish their goal?" (Joyce Lee, Human Factors Design at Apple).

Let's look at the who, the what, the why, and the how of usability testing.

The Who

When considering who might be using your products or services, recruiting people with disabilities can help you get a better understanding of the use of your product. With the broad range of disabilities out there, we will focus on the ones here:

- Visual: Legally blind and low vision

- Auditory: Legally deaf

- Motor: Heavy usage of keyboard and/or other peripherals.

- Cognitive: Focus, perception

- Speech: Unable to use voice

When you're choosing the number of participants for your test, it is important to have an appropriately representative sample based on the medium or artifact you are testing (i.e., the number is a sliding scale). The following is a sample recruitment plan illustrating which categories of disability to include in your usability test depending on the medium or artifact you are testing:

1. Testing a media application (e.g., YouTube): Visual, low vision, cognitive (focus), cognitive (perception), motor, and auditory

2. Online retail (e.g., Target): Visual, low vision, cognitive (focus), cognitive (perception), motor, and auditory

3. Gaming company (e.g., Nintendo): Motor, visual, low vision, cognitive (focus), cognitive (perception), and auditory. For example, if you are designing a/ for a rumble pad and the game itself (i.e., you are testing both hardware and software)

Figure 9-2 shows a chart of Category, Parameters, Test Subject, Disability and Notes from Deque.

Category	Test Subject Parameters	Disability	Notes
Visual (Blind)	Screen reader only (does not use vision for tasks)	• No Light perception • Light perception • Legally Blind	By testing with a screen reader who does not use vision for these tasks, we efficiently and effectively cover all three of these use cases.
Low Vision	Screen Magnifier User (with visual acuity between 20/70 and 20/200) that uses 4x to 6x magnification.	Visual acuity between 20/70 and 20/200 in the better-seeing eye with best conventional correction.	
Auditory	User who relies on captions/transcripts (not audio)	• Deaf • Hard of hearing	Only required if there is audio content

Figure 9-2.   Chart of Category, Parameters, Test Subject, Disability and Notes from Deque www.deque.com/blog/considering-accessibility-when-designing-a-usability-test/

Motor	Sighted user who only uses a keyboard. User with a tremor frequency of multiple tremors per second in the body part that is used to interact with technology	• No hands • Paralysis • Reduced dexterity • Tremors	
Cognitive (Perception)	User has documented diagnosis for dyslexia that took regular courses in K12 or Higher Ed.	Dyslexia	A single user may have multiple cognitive disabilities. That user may be counted as filling multiple categories.
Cognitive (Focus)	User that has/had a documented 504 plan (or doctor's diagnosis) for focus issues that took regular courses in K12 or Higher Ed.	Attention disorders	A single user may have multiple cognitive disabilities. That user may be counted as filling multiple categories.

Figure 9-2. (*continued*)

The What

When conducting usability tests, it is not recommended to conduct tasks with the following disability types:

- Color blindness—Use trusted scientific methods/tools to reliably ensure that the content meets the needs of the colorblind.

- Cognitive (seizure)—Use trusted scientific methods/tools to reliably ensure that the content does not cause seizures. Instead, use trusted scientific methods/tools to reliably ensure that the content does not cause seizures.

- Speech—Only required if voice control is the only method of computer interaction.

Use caution when including the following disability types:

- Cognitive (memory)—CAUTION: Some complex online tasks or complex interfaces may be overwhelming. If you conduct usability studies for people with memory issues, there is a risk that some complex tasks could cause cognitive overload problems.

- Cognitive (executive function)—CAUTION: Some complex online tasks or complex interfaces may be overwhelming. If you conduct usability studies for people with executive function disorders, there is a risk that some complex tasks could cause cognitive overload problems.

After your company screens, validates, and recruits for the following disability types and schedule the participants, note that the average no-show rate is around 11%. To minimize this rate, you may want to offer a monetary incentive to participants for their participation.[1]

In general, recruitment for usability testing can come with various opportunities and will give you the chance to explore options you may not have tried before. When recruiting, you will want to think about who you will need to participate and plan accordingly.

If you work with an external recruiter ask them if they have experience recruiting people with disabilities; some do. If you are recruiting internally (without an external recruiter), you may need to reach out to organizations that have access to people with disabilities. For example, if you need to recruit participants with visually disabilities in the United States, you should contact a local chapter of the National Federation of the Blind (`https://nfb.org/state-and-local-organizations`) or local training centers. If you use social media to advertise your study, a good approach is to use the hashtag #a11y (stands for accessibility—there are 11 letters between the "a" and "y") in your post.[2]

We have discussed who, now let's see some reasons why usability testing is important.

The Why

Accessibility is the right thing to do. And not just the right thing; it's profoundly the right thing to do, because the one argument for accessibility that doesn't get made nearly often enough is how extraordinarily better it makes some people's lives. How many opportunities do we have to dramatically improve people's lives just by doing our job a little better?

—Steve Krug

---

[1]Deque—Consider accessibility when conducting usability testing `www.deque.com/blog/considering-accessibility-when-designing-a-usability-test/`

[2]Smashing Magazine—Tips for conducting usability studies with participants with disabilities `www.smashingmagazine.com/2018/03/tips-conducting-usability-studies-participants-disabilities/`

The benefits of usability testing can far outweigh the costs. Behind anything we do is the "why," why do we need to test with people with disabilities? Here are a few of the reasons why usability testing is important:

1. You can increase overall user experience by providing options for a wide range of human abilities.

2. Increase the number of people who can access your product or service.

3. Increase market share and brand recognition.

4. Find problems with interactions that internal testing could not identify.

5. It's the right thing to do!

Besides this list, there are many other reasons for usability testing that you can discuss internally with your team and your stakeholders. Launching a product or service can cost a lot of time and money. To make the most of your time and money, consider the benefits to your organization. In this next section, we will discuss what needs to be done for usability testing.

> *When UX doesn't consider ALL users, shouldn't it be known as "SOME User Experience" or... SUX?*
>
> —Billy Gregory, Senior Accessibility Engineer

Outlining a plan for your usability testing will help you figure out what you will need as well as the steps that need to be taken to ensure the objectives of the usability test are met. Before testing your product with users, you will want to conduct a quality check of your product before its release. From your perspective, everything may work perfectly, but the reason for that may be that you know the product very well. You will want to see if your users can do what they need to do to accomplish the things you think they should. Always keep in mind that you are not your user.

It's not Me X, it's UX.

—Aaron Neeley, Product Designer and Educator

Table 9-1 provides an example of what a usability test plan might look like on a high level. A good resource for a more in-depth plan can be found at Usability.gov.

Table 9-1. *Sample usability test plan*

Category	Questions to ask
Objective or purpose	Why are you testing?
Responsibilities	Who is responsible for what on the team? Will you have a facilitator?
Participants	Who are you testing with? How will your recruit people for usability testing?
Methods	What type of methodology will you use? Lab test, field tests?
Tasks	What tasks will your user need to complete?
Inputs/outputs	What needs to be input into the product? What is expected to come out?
Premortem (risk assessments)	Document all the things that can go wrong
Time frame	How long do you expect the test to last? How long will you test, for days, weeks, months?

Table 9-2 provides an example of a testing plan for a mobile application.

Table 9-2. *Mobile app testing plan*

Category	Description
Objective or purpose	• Understand if mobile application can be used by people with various levels of ability.
Responsibilities	• 1 observer and 1 notetaker
Participants	• 40 participants • Participants will receive a gift card as an incentive to complete the test
Methods	• Usability test at office with user, observer and notetaker in room. • User will be assigned a task to complete. • Sessions will be recorded for later review
Tasks	• User will be asked to follow verbal script • Sign up for app • Use search functionality of app
Inputs/outputs	• Inputs: User will input name, email and likes and dislikes • Output: Prioritization of issues found
Premortem (risk assessments)	• User is not able to log in • User is not able to search • App freezes and the user is not able to move forward
Time frame	• 30-minute sessions for app use, 30-minute interview post app use • 4 weeks of usability testing for 40 participants

After you've conducted usability testing, you will be left with information to move forward with your design and development. Research synthesis involves gathering all you've discovered, looking for patterns and bringing that infomation together. Prioritizing what needs to be addressed first and sequencing issues to be addressed could also be added to the synthesis.

The following section provides a usability case study.

Accessibility Originates with UX: A BBC iPlayer Case Study

Design with choice in mind, and always give users control over the page. In this article, Henny Swan shares key principles that will ensure that your products are inclusive and usable for disabled people.

Not long after I started working at the BBC, I fielded a complaint from a screen reader user who was having trouble finding a favorite show via the BBC iPlayer's home page (Figure 9-3). The web site had recently undergone an independent accessibility audit which indicated that, other than the odd minor issue here and there, it was reasonably accessible.

I called the customer to establish what exactly the problem was, and together we navigated the home page using a screen reader. It was at that point I realized that, while all of the traditional ingredients of an accessible page were in place—headings, WAI ARIA Landmarks, text alternatives, and so on—it wasn't very usable for a screen reader user.

Figure 9-3. *BBC iPlayer's home page*

The first issue was that the subnavigation was made up of only two links: "TV" and "Radio," with links to other key areas such as "Categories," "Channels," and "A to Z" buried further down the content order of the page, making them harder for the user to find.

Primary
information
placed too far
down the page

Figure 9-4. *iPlayer's old home page showing "Categories,"*
"Channels," and "A to Z" far down the content order

The second issue was how verbose the page was to the screen reader
user. Instead of hearing a link to a program once, the program would be
announced twice because the thumbnail image and the heading for the
program were presented as two separate links (Figure 9-5).

This made the page longer to listen to and was confusing because links
to the same destination were worded differently.

Link
overload

Figure 9-5. *iPlayer's old home page showing duplicate links*

Finally, keyboard access on the page was illogical. In the "Categories" area, for example, a single click on a category would reveal four items in a panel next to it (Figure 9-6). To access the full list of items in that category, you had to click again on the same link to be taken to a listing page. This was a major hurdle for the user and the place where the customer I was talking to gave up using the application altogether.

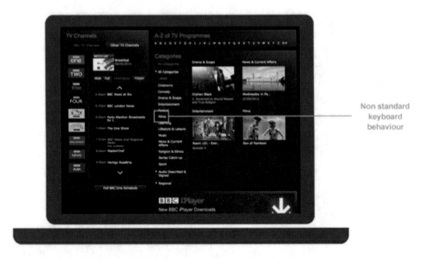

Figure 9-6. iPlayer's old home page showing the "Categories" links highlighted

It was clear that, while the web site had been built with accessibility in mind, it hadn't been designed with accessibility in mind, and this is where the issues originated.

The Challenge

At the BBC, a number of internal standards and guidelines are in place that teams are required to follow when delivering accessible web site and mobile applications. Key ones are

- Accessibility standards and guidelines
- Screen reader testing guidelines,
- Mobile accessibility standards and guidelines

There is also a strong culture of accessibility; the BBC is a publicly funded organization, and accessibility is considered central to its remit and is a stronger driver than any legal requirement. So, how did this happen?

Part of the issue is that standards and guidelines tend to focus more on code than design, more on output than outcome, and more on compliance than experience. As such, technically compliant pages could be built that are not the most usable for disabled users.

It may not seem immediately obvious, but visual design can have a massive impact on users who cannot see the page. I often find that mobile applications and web sites that are problematic to make accessible are the ones where the visual design, by dictating structure, does not allow it.

This does not mean that standards and guidelines are redundant—far from it. But what we have found at the BBC is that standards need to sit within, and inform, an accessibility framework that runs through product management, user experience, development, and quality assurance. As such, accessibility originates with UX. Most of the thinking and requirements should be considered up front so that poor accessibility isn't designed in.

While redesigning the BBC iPlayer web site, renewed focus was given to inclusive design, which, while adhering to the BBC's standards and guidelines, is driven by four principles (more on that later). We then distilled our standards and guidelines to create a focused list of requirements for the UX to follow. We also started to train designers to annotate their own designs for accessibility.

UX Principles

Our four main principles are the following:

- Give users choice
- Put users in control
- Design with familiarity in mind
- Prioritize features that add value

Give Users Choice

Never assume that just because a user can access content one way that they want to access content in that one way. Because BBC's iPlayer has "audio described" and "sign language" formats, it was never in any doubt that both of these should have their own dedicated listing pages, accessed via the "Categories" dropdown link (Figure 9-7). (Note that all on-demand content is subtitled, which is why there is no "Subtitled" category. Subtitles can be switched on in the media player.)

Figure 9-7. *The "Categories" dropdown with "Audio Described" and "Signed" sections*

User research and feedback indicated, however, that although people want dedicated categories, they also want to be able to search for and browse content in the same way that any other users would and to select their preferred format from there (Figure 9-8). I have stayed in touch over the years with the gentleman who complained about the old iPlayer page, and he's said himself, "Don't send us into disability silos!"

This means that from the outset, the designs need to signpost "Audio Description" and "Signed" content via search results, A to Z, category, and other listing pages. Not making any assumptions or not stereotyping users with disabilities is important—for instance, a person with a severe vision impairment might not always use audio descriptions; news, sports, music programs, and live events often aren't supported by audio description because commentators already provide enriched commentary.

Figure 9-8. *List pages such as search, shown here, indicate what formats programs are available in*

On-demand pages also list alternative formats, allowing users to choose what they want. Looking ahead, the option to choose your format could also be included in the Standard Media Player—the BBC media player used for on-demand and live streaming video across all BBC products, including iPlayer (Figure 9-9).

Figure 9-9. *Playback page showing HD and AD formats*

Put Users in Control

Never taking control away from the user is essential. A key aspect of this in iPlayer, which is responsive, is not suppressing pinch zoom. Time and again in user testing, we have observed users zooming content, even on responsive web sites, where text might be intentionally larger.

Due to an iOS bug that was rectified in iOS 6, the ability to pinch zoom was suppressed on many web sites due to poor resizing when the orientation is changed from portrait to landscape. Now that this has been fixed, there is no reason to continue suppressing zoom.

Another aspect of control is autoplay. While iPlayer currently has autoplay for live content, this can be a problem because the sound of the video can make it difficult for a screen reader user to hear their reader's output. However, we do know of screen reader users who request autoplay because it means they don't have to navigate to the player, find the play button, and activate play. The answer is to look at ways to give users control over playback by opting in or out of autoplay, such as by using a popup and saving preferences with cookies.

Design with Familiarity in Mind

There needs to be a balance between the new and the familiar. Users understand how to interact with pages and apps that use familiar design patterns. This is especially important in native apps for iOS and Android, where standard UI components come with accessibility built in.

Equally important is the language used across the BBC's native iPlayer apps and responsive web site. Where the platform allows, consistent labels for headings, links, and buttons—not just visually but also via alternatives for screen reader users—ensure that the experience is familiar and recognizably "BBC iPlayer," regardless of the platform.

Tied into this, the new designs reinforce a logical heading structure within the code, which in turn supports navigation for screen reader users. Key to this is ensuring that the pattern used for the heading structure is repeated across pages, so that users do not find main headings in different places depending on what page they are on. While structure is typically viewed as a responsibility of developers, it needs to be decided before designs are signed off in order to prevent poor structure getting coded in—more on that later.

Prioritize Features That Add Value

Accessibility at the BBC is not just about meeting code, content, and design requirements but also about incorporating helpful features that add value for all users, including disabled users. A large proportion of feedback we get from our disabled users pertains to usability issues that could be experienced by anyone on some level but that seriously adversely affect disabled users. When we incorporate features to help users with specific disabilities, everyone gains access to a richer and easier experience.

One obstacle that comes up time and again is finding a favorite show. I've spoken with many screen reader users who say they save shortcuts to their favorite shows on their desktop but, due to changing URLs, often lose content. A simple way to address this that benefits all users is to ensure that there is a mechanism for saving favorites on the web site. Adding in options to sort favorites and list them the way you want further improves this. It may sound unrelated to accessibility, but it was the single most requested feature received from disabled users. Simply accessing the favorites page to watch the latest episode of something, rather than having to search the web site, makes all the difference (Figure 9-10).

Figure 9-10. *The "Favorites" page, with options to sort by "A to Z" and "Recent"*

Finding ways to allow people to get to the content they want more quickly has also influenced what is available within the media player itself. Once an episode has finished playing, exiting the media player and navigating back to the web site to find the next episode is a massive overhead for some users (Figure 9-11). Adding a "More" button to the player itself—showing the next episode or programs similar to the current one—cuts down on the amount of effort it takes users to find new content.

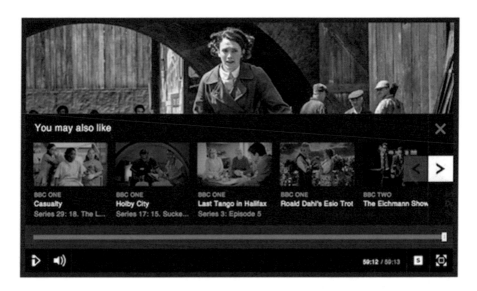

Figure 9-11. *The "You may also like" plugin shows related content and next episodes within the Standard Media Player*

One key feature that has added value to BBC iPlayer's native iOS and Android apps, as well as the web site (when viewed in Chrome), is support for Google Chromecast (Figure 9-12). Being able to control what content you view on TV without having to use a remote or complex TV user interface is invaluable. Using one's device of choice, whether it be iOS or Android, is much easier for a disabled user than using a remote control and a potentially inaccessible TV interface.

Figure 9-12. *BBC iPlayer and Chromecast*

Guidelines

The preceding principles exist to create a mindset that helps product owners and UX practitioners alike when shaping and designing inclusive products. In addition to the four principles, a set of guidelines is used to design more accessible interfaces. The following are a subset taken from the "BBC Mobile Accessibility Standards and Guidelines":

1. Color contrast
   Ensure that text and backgrounds exceed the WCAG Double A 4.5:1 contrast minimum.

2. Color and meaning
   Information conveyed with color must also be identifiable from context or markup.

3. Content order
   Content order must be logical.

4. Structure
    When supported by the platform, pages must
    provide a logical and hierarchical heading structure.

5. Containers and landmarks
    When supported by the platform, page containers
    or landmarks should be used to describe page
    structure.

6. Duplicate links
    Controls, objects, and grouped interface elements
    must be represented as a single component.

7. Touch target size
    Targets must be large enough to touch accurately
    (44 pixels).

8. Spacing
    An inactive space must surround all active elements
    (unless they are large blocks exceeding 44 pixels).

9. Zoom
    Where zoom is supported by the platform, it must
    not be suppressed.

10. Actionable elements
    Links and other actionable elements must be clearly
    distinguishable.

The New IPlayer

Keeping in mind this backdrop of principles and guidelines, along with the
renewed focus on adding value and features that enhance the experience
for disabled users, here are a few of the changes introduced in the BBC's
new iPlayer (Figure 9-13).

Primary information at top of screen

Better search and discover tools

Managed keyboard access

Figure 9-13. *The BBC's new iPlayer home page has better content order, search tools, structure, and keyboard access*

At launch, the iPlayer's navigation housed BBC's channels, a "TV Guide," "Favourites," and "Categories." These all sit at the start of the page, high up in the content order. While they are visually easy to see, they are also easily discoverable by screen reader users via a hidden heading and labeled navigation landmark:

```
<div role="navigation">
<h2>iPlayer navigation</h2>
```

Copy

Where previously the "Categories" were unusable for the screen reader user I spoke with, they are now prominent in the page and fully keyboard navigable. Since launch, the addition of more channels has meant that the channel links have been rehoused in their own dropdown menu.

Search tools have also been added, enabling users to carry out predictive search, browse A to Z or view their most recently watched program. This is all keyboard accessible, it makes use of headings, and it has landmarks where appropriate.

The home page carousel is also fully keyboard accessible. Each program in the stream is presented as one link, with the reading order of text starting with the primary information first: channel attribution, program name, episode information, abstract, and program duration.

Work has also been carried out to improve visible focus and bring both the iPlayer web site and the Standard Media Player in line with the BBC header and footer. The pink underline used for the hover and focus states in the main BBC navigation is now used within the Standard Media Player to indicate when a button is selected (Figure 9-14) for example, when the subtitles are switched on. This replaces the use of color only to indicate a selected state, which was indistinguishable from the hover and focus states (Figure 9-15).

Figure 9-14. *The hover and focus pink underline used in the BBC header for iPlayer*

Figure 9-15. *Active and inactive hover and focus states on the subtitle button in the Standard Media Player*

Annotated UX

All of the thinking around inclusive design that comes from product owners, UX practitioners and designers need to be captured and communicated to developers and engineers. At the BBC, we are moving to a model where designs need to be annotated for accessibility. This includes

- Headings

- Containers

- Content order

- Color contrast

- Alternatives to color and meaning

- Visible focus

- Keyboard and input interactions

The design in Figure 9-16 shows an early version of the BBC One home page in iPlayer, outlines where the <h1> to <h6> headings should be.

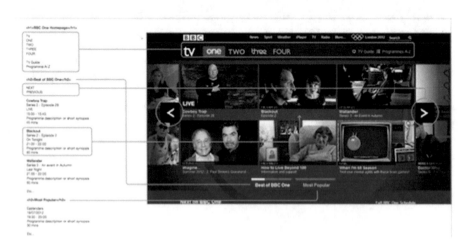

Figure 9-16. *Annotated UX showing headings and labels*

The UX practitioner doesn't need an in-depth knowledge of code, but rather an understanding of the hierarchy of data within a page. As such, an equally acceptable approach would be to indicate the "main heading," "secondary heading," "third-level heading," and so on. Developers can then take this and translate it into semantic markup.

Equally, indicating the logical order of content helps developers to code content in the right sequence (i.e., source order)—something that is essential to a screen reader or sighted keyboard user's comprehension of the page.

Annotating the UX in this way is key to identifying designs that don't allow for a logical page structure, content order, or behavior. It is the first step to generating a style guide that documents focus states, colors, and so on. Further down the line, these requirements can also be used to generate user acceptance criteria and automated quality assurance tests.

Even if you're working in an agile way, where designs are iterative and not delivered in a complete form, annotation still works. As long as the basic framework of the page is well defined, the visual design can evolve from that.

It's very easy to get bogged down by accessible output and to forget that, ultimately, accessibility is about people. As such, keep the following in mind, whether you are working in product, UX, development, or quality assurance:

- Design with choice in mind.

- Always give users control over the page.

- Prioritize features that add value for disabled users.

- Design with familiarity in mind.

- Integrate accessibility into annotated UX and style guides.

- Make no assumptions. Test ideas and concepts.

Fostering these key principles across the entire team will go a long way to ensuring that products are inclusive and usable for disabled people. Listening to users and actively including their feedback, along with adhering to organizational standards and guidelines, are essential.[3]

Conclusion

The BBC case study is an example of usability of an existing product that was initially built with accessibility in mind but did not meet the marks of all the accessibility standards that had been put in place by the organization. By understanding the existing gaps in usability, they were able to create a framework that was more usable. Making something accessible doesn't mean that it is usable. It is imperative that usability testing be conducted with people with disabilities to ensure that you are making products and services inclusive.

Remember the who, what, and why of usability testing. For further reading on usability testing, there are additional resources in the appendix.

There are many factors involved in usability testing and having a plan is key. Testing the product internally and externally can help with the success of your product. Usability testing is a way for you to get real-world feedback that can be applied to making your product better and more usable.

Usability testing takes time in effort in terms of planning, recruiting participants, and analyzing the results. When possible, consult with usability professionals to help facilitate the process .

In order to understand where we come from and where we are going, looking at past innovations and work can help us determine where it is possible to go. In Chapter 10, we look at past innovations, present technologies, and future opportunities.

---

[3]Accessibility originates with UX: A BBC iPlayer Case Study www.smashingmagazine.com/2015/02/bbc-iplayer-accessibility-case-study/

CHAPTER 10

Beyond the Web

*Inclusive Design is a methodology, born out of digital environ-
ments, that enables and draws on the full range of human
diversity. Most importantly, this means including and learning from people with a range of perspectives.*

—Microsoft

Reminding ourselves that we all are temporarily able-bodied is a good
way to remember that you don't want to be left out of doing the day-to-day
things you might do now. If we truly want to be inclusive with the products
we create, we have to look beyond ourselves and look at creating things for
a wider range of people.

Looking back at past innovations can inspire us to create for the
future. Many past innovations have been created for and by people with
disabilities, and many of these innovations have benefited more than
the disabled community. Let's take a look at some of the ones that were
inspired or created by people with disabilities.

The Phone

The telephone was invented by Alexander Graham Bell in the United
States in the 1870s. Bell's mother had progressive deafness and this led
him to study acoustics. Bell's father worked to teach deaf people to speak,

R. M. Gilbert, *Inclusive Design for a Digital World*,
https://doi.org/10.1007/978-1-4842-5016-7_10

an approach considered groundbreaking at the time. In their youth, Bell and his brothers learned to write visible speech (symbols showing lip movements to sounds) and to match symbols to their correlating sound.

As an adult, Bell studied sound and its creation. He used the telegraph as a basis for inventing the telephone. On October 9, 1876, the first phone conversation took place between Bell and Thomas A. Watson. A year later, the Bell Telephone Company was created, and by 1886, over 150,000 people in the United States had phones (remember, the Internet runs over phone lines).

> *Accessibility is not a feature, is a social trend.*
>
> —Antonio Santos

The Internet

Vinton Cerf, Google's chief evangelist, was central to creating the early Internet. Cerf is hard of hearing and in the 1970s was part of an initial research team into Internet protocols under Steve Crocker. Cerf's hearing issues meant he needed to share documents with associates instead of talking on a phone. The first IP-based network resulted in 1981 and has evolved into today's sophisticated telecom networks.

Only since the early 1990s has the Internet been a portal for online communication and social networking.

Text Messaging

Have you sent a text message today? If so, you are using something that was originally made for people who are deaf. The first SMS (short message service) was sent in 1992. The idea of SMS was first discussed by Matti Makkonen in a Copenhagen pizzeria with two others, Seppo Tiainen and Juhani Tapiol. Makkonen invented SMS texting for deaf people to communicate, but when SMS offered an incredible new method for saving telecom bandwidth, the world of cellular telecommunications changed.[1] And now we all benefit from this technological invention.

Technology Designed for Disabled People Can Help Everyone

The "curb cut" effect refers to actual sidewalk "curb cuts," an innovation that was implemented throughout the 1970s and 1980s (Figure 10-1). It is now a requirement after the 1990 Americans with Disabilities Act.

---

[1]Deafness lead to the phone, Internet, and SMS `https://sound-advice.ie/ deaf-phone-internet-sms-text/`

Figure 10-1. *NYC Curb Cut with tactile warning surface*

As it turned out, the invention was a net benefit to not only those with physical limitations but everyone else, too. "When the wall of exclusion came down, everybody benefited – not only people in wheelchairs. Parents pushing strollers headed straight for the curb cuts. So did workers pushing heavy carts, business travelers wheeling luggage, even runners and skateboarders." Along with curb cuts are tactile warnings which are the raised bumps that can be seen and felt.

In design principles, this is referred to as "universal design." The underpinnings of universal design suggest that developing a product or service that meets the needs of extreme user types will be a product that appeals to more users overall. Indeed, the curb cut or ramp does not prohibit anyone who already had the ability to use the stairs.[2]

Cruise Control

Do you drive a car? Have you ever used cruise control? Did you know it was invented by a person who was blind? Ralph Teetor invented a common automotive feature known as cruise control.

If you drive a modern vehicle with an automatic steering option, chances are you've also used speed control or the cruise control feature of your vehicle once in a while. Most vehicles today are configured to maintain an average speed automatically in order to save fuel and make driving a more convenient and safer experience.

Cruise control, as this feature is commonly known, was invented as a solution to a very common inconvenience which Ralph Teetor hated: irregular speeds. His own lawyer was guilty of slowing down and speeding up as he talked; this annoyed Teetor but later gave him the idea of

---

[2]The Curb Cut Effect: How Making Public Spaces Accessible to People With Disabilities Helps Everyone `https://medium.com/@mosaicofminds/the-curb-cut-effect-how-making-public-spaces-accessible-to-people-with-disabilities-helps-everyone-d69f24c58785`

designing an automated function that would maintain speeds in cars. The result is the automatic speed control feature found in most cars today.

Cruise control was first installed in 1958 on several Chrysler models, but by 1960, it was a common feature in all Cadillacs. The amazing thing about creating something is that it is often created by a problem that could be big or small.

Screen Readers

Another innovation that has been discussed throughout the book is screen readers. One such screen reader NVDA was created by James Teh and Michael Curran. Teh and Curran invented a useful voice-to-speech system known as NVDA or NonVisual Desktop Access which "reads" text on a computer screen dependent on mouse movement.

Both James Teh and Michael Curran suffer from visual impairment to a certain degree, but you would be surprised to know that these two gentlemen still managed to create a voice-to-speech program that aims to assist blind computer users with their day-to-day computer usage. NVDA or the NonVisual Desktop Access program has been considered a technological breakthrough for the blind by many outlets, and the best part about this program is that it's free.

Basically, NVDA "reads" whatever your mouse touches on your computer screen. If you hover your mouse over the start menu, the program will tell you that you are now touching the "Start" button.

The audio instructions of the NVDA have helped blind computer users use computers independently and to their full extent. In fact, around 1.5 computer power-users, or computer users who are online for more than 8 hours per day, today are actually visually impaired.

Unlike other speech readers that require customized computer gears in order to function properly, NVDA is an independent program that does not require any specific hardware to function. That means, you can use NVDA with a regular QWERTY keyboard and even an ergonomic keyboard and it should work just as fine.[3]

Inventions Out of Necessity

Many of the past innovations came out of necessity, annoyance, and curiosity. And the audience for many of the creations stems beyond the communities they were built for. The opportunities for us to build more usable and accessible products are endless. It takes being able to see what others have accomplished in order for us to get some ideas for what we might create. In 2017, the Cooper Hewitt Museum had an exhibit called Access + Ability which showed some amazing inventions of accessibility.

Access + Ability at the Cooper Hewitt

The Cooper Hewitt Museum in New York, New York, held an exhibit from December 15, 2017, to September 3, 2018. It was an exhibit I got to experience and opened my eyes to the many innovations that are possible (Figure 10-2).

In a statement, the museum said, "We are experiencing a surge of design with and by people who span a wide range of physical, cognitive, and sensory abilities." Fueled by advances in research and technology, the proliferation of functional, life-enhancing products is creating unprecedented access in homes, schools, workplaces, and the world at large.

---

[3] 7 Life Changing Inventions Created by Blind Inventors `https://owlcation.com/humanities/7-Life-Changing-Inventions-Created-by-Blind-Inventors`

The significant improvements have been motivated by several factors: the Americans with Disabilities Act of 1990—amended in 2008—prohibiting discrimination against people with disabilities, increased advocacy demanding greater accessibility and inclusivity, a worldwide aging population, and unprecedented communication possibilities due to digital technologies. Designers have responded to these technical and social changes with multidisciplinary creative approaches that are both user-centered and inclusive.

When the design process encompasses individuals with diverse abilities and background, the shortcomings of existing products and environments often become the catalyst for design breakthroughs. The objects and experiences featured in this exhibition were selected based on input from users first and foremost, as well as designers, caregivers, activists, researchers, occupational therapists, neuroscientists, and others whose knowledge is inspiring opportunities for design to flourish.

Most of the works are in production, but some are prototypes that point to future directions in this rapidly advancing realm of design. Many of the best solutions have and will continue to come from the ingenuity of people who develop, adapt, and customize designs to fit their specific challenges, needs, and aesthetics.[4]

---

[4]Access + Accessibility https://collection.cooperhewitt.org/exhibitions/1141959921/

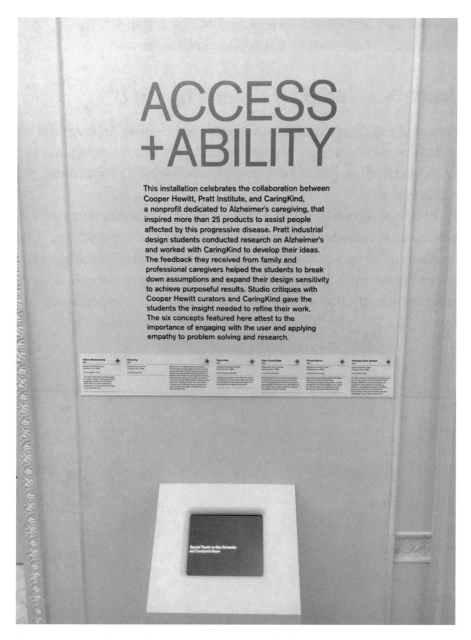

Figure 10-2. *Entry Sign for Access and Ability at the Cooper Hewitt Museum*

Here are a few of the items for accessibility that can/have the opportunity to increase the way people operate in the world.

Vision Aid, BrainPort Vision Pro, 2017

Vision Aid was designed by Wicab, Inc. (see Figure 10-3). Although it is not part of Cooper Hewitt's permanent collection, it was at the museum on loan from Wicab, as part of Access+Ability. Its medium is polycarbonate plastic cables.

BrainPort is based on the proposition that one sees with the brain, not with the eyes. Embedded in the headset is a camera, a surrogate "eye," that translates the shapes of things in the physical world into vibrations that can be felt through a device placed on the user's tongue. With practice, one can learn to interpret the vibrating patterns and actually start to see.[5]

---

[5]Vision Aid https://collection.cooperhewitt.org/objects/1158794687/

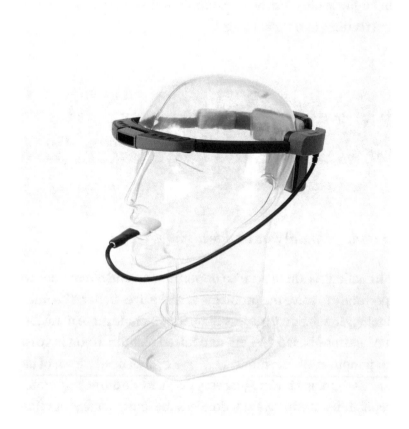

Figure 10-3. *Vision Aid*

Braille Display, HumanWare Brailliant BI 40, 2011

Figure 10-4 shows a braille display. It was designed by HumanWare. It is dated 2011. Its medium is aluminum and plastic. This small and portable HumanWare Brailliant braille Display essentially puts braille at one's fingertips. Used in conjunction with a laptop, tablet, or mobile device, the keyboard's simple layout has braille input and output, and is particularly efficient for navigating text-heavy communication such as writing emails, extensive reading, and note taking.[6]

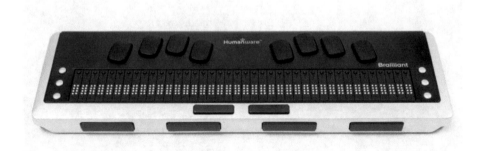

Figure 10-4. *HumanWare braille display*

With challenges, there are also opportunities, and as creators, we have the opportunity to solve the problems to make lives better. The future of technology in relation to accessibility may include more in relation to haptics, gesture-based designs, and mixed realities. If you have ever put your phone on vibrate mode, you have experienced a form of haptic feedback. Technology is changing very fast, and we are seeing more and more capabilities of what we can do. Sky's the limit; our sky, our limit. Let's explore some future applications of technology and accessibility.

Future of Mixed Realities and Accessibility

When we think of what the future looks like for us, virtual experiences may come to mind. Virtual reality, augmented reality, and mixed realities are often spoken about, and here are some definitions of each of the areas for further clarity.

---

[6]Braille Display from HumanWare `https://collection.cooperhewitt.org/` `objects/1158817803/`

Virtual Reality (VR)

VR is the most widely known of these technologies. It is fully immersive, which tricks your senses into thinking you're in a different environment or world apart from the real world. Using a head-mounted display (HMD) or headset, you'll experience a computer-generated world of imagery and sounds in which you can manipulate objects and move around using haptic controllers while tethered to a console or PC.

Augmented Reality (AR)

AR overlays digital information on real-world elements. Pokémon GO is among the best-known examples. Augmented reality keeps the real world central but enhances it with other digital details, layering new strata of perception, and supplementing your reality or environment.

Mixed Reality (MR)

MR brings together real-world and digital elements. In mixed reality, you interact with and manipulate both physical and virtual items and environments, using next-generation sensing and imaging technologies. Mixed reality allows you to see and immerse yourself in the world around you even as you interact with a virtual environment using your own hands—all without ever removing your headset. It provides the ability to have one foot (or hand) in the real world and the other in an imaginary place, breaking down basic concepts between real and imaginary, offering an experience that can change the way you game and work today.

Using Virtual Reality Technologies

From gaming to movies, to medicine, the uses for virtual reality, augmented reality, and mixed reality are expanding into the following areas:

- **Healthcare**—For training, such as for surgical simulations

- **Film and TV**—For movies and shows to create unique experiences

- **Virtual travel**—For virtual trips to an art museum—or another planet—all from home

- **Professional sports**—For training programs like STRIVR to help pro and amateur athletes

- **Gaming**—For over 1,000 games already available, from first-person shooters to strategy games to role-playing adventures

Headsets

There are many, many VR headsets available, all with varying performance levels and prices. Entry-level gear, such as Google Cardboard, uses your mobile phone as the screen, whereas PC-operated devices, like the HTC Vive or Oculus Rift, are immersive—providing a premium VR environment.

Some AR headsets are available on the market today, with more rumored to be coming in the future. The Microsoft Hololens, Google Glass, Magic Leap and the Meta 2 headset are great examples. Every PC-connected HMD will have different system requirements, so if you're buying a new virtual reality headset, make sure you check with the HMD (Head Mounted Display) vendor for their recommended and minimum system requirements.

Computers

If you are looking for a new computer and you're interested in VR, you'll need something that can handle heavy loads. When it comes to high-end desktops or laptops for virtual reality (and other advanced tasks like gaming or video editing), the CPU, GPU, and memory are the most critical components.

Without these high-performing components working in sync, you could have a pretty miserable experience. A powerful system will ensure that you'll have fun as you lean in, stand up, or walk around. VR that lags makes it impossible for the virtual world to respond as you expect, which can lead to more than just disappointment; it increases the risk of motion sickness. A high-end processor assists in positional tracking and controls how real and immersive your virtual environment will be, so you'll enjoy a deeper experience in a higher-fidelity environment.

A discrete graphics processing unit (GPU) is recommended, or in the case of Oculus Rift, HTC Vive, and Windows Mixed Reality Ultra, it is required. The GPU is responsible for rendering the high-resolution, immersive images needed for VR. Oculus, HTC, and Microsoft all have profiler tools that you can download from their web sites, and you can use to run on your PC to determine if it meets the minimum requirements for their VR headsets.

Choose Your Experience

New VR and AR technologies and products continue to come to market, making new environments accessible to the masses. Virtual, Augmented, Mixed—the choice for a new reality is up to you. Let your imagination, and your readiness to try new gear, enhance your experience![7] With the emergence of these technologies, there is still some ways to go in order to make them more accessible. There are many universities and organizations working on making mixed reality experiences more accessible. The following sections review a few examples of what is to come.

Education and Skill Teaching

One of the most significant problems that many people with disability face is a lack of independence, mainly when handling day-to-day affairs. For example, some studies have explored the potential use of virtual reality in teaching people with autism-specific life skills necessary to lead more independent lives. In one such study, researchers used virtual reality training programs to teach autistic children how to cross roads safely. After a month-long exercise, researchers established that virtual reality training significantly improved the ability of the children to cross the road.

Even recently disabled people can use virtual reality training to learn how to navigate through traffic and other situations using a wheelchair.

Additionally, people with disabilities that negatively impact their social skills can use virtual reality to practice and improve their social skills.

Perhaps the most exciting application of virtual reality is in fighting stigma and reducing the general misunderstanding regarding what people with disabilities go through. Educators can use virtual reality to help people get an almost "first-hand" experience of what people with

---

[7]Demystifying the Virtual Landscape www.intel.com/content/www/us/en/tech-tips-and-tricks/virtual-reality-vs-augmented-reality.html

conditions such as autism, epilepsy, and Alzheimer's among others go through. One of the best examples of this application is a smartphone application dedicated to providing those without the disability, the feeling of living in an autistic home. Some virtual reality software also simulates life with schizophrenia.

New and Formerly "Impossible" Experiences

Disability often makes it difficult for people to try out specific experiences. For example, it is difficult for a person in a wheelchair to climb to the top of Mount Everest or even engage in activities such as skydiving or skateboarding. With virtual reality, however, disabled people can experience all these activities and more. Indeed, many disabled individuals have expressed pleasure in experiencing activities such as virtual surfing or even visiting space virtually. Such experiences will improve the mental and physical health of the disabled individuals.

Route Planning

When visiting new places, it is often difficult for physically disabled people to plan on routes to use around a city. Virtual reality can help provide a simulated environment of the city and thus allow the disabled individual to have a feel of the city and get "accustomed" to the most accessible routes to use.

Motor Skills and Muscle Recovery

Virtual reality is also useful in helping people who have suffered from strokes or sports-related injuries and even vestibular system issues to improve their motor skills and help in muscle recovery. According to research, even the act of imagining that one is performing an activity is enough to stimulate the relevant parts of the brain needed to perform the activity.

Improved Gaming Experiences for Deaf People

It is also possible to use virtual reality in combination with other technologies such as special gloves to provide richer gaming experiences for deaf people. This is made possible through the translation of sign language into audio or text within a game or within the virtual reality environment. Deaf people could, therefore, interact better with speaking characters and speaking people.

Clearer Vision

Some conditions such as Stargardt's disease can lead to visual impairment in the form of reduced central detailed vision. However, research has established that it is possible to use VR to help people with such visual disabilities see images with greater clarity.

Although there is immense potential in augmented and virtual reality industry, it is important to note that it is still relatively young and undeveloped. In addition to that, little is known about the long-term effects of AR and VR on the mental and physical health of users. Researchers are particularly concerned about the long-term effects of AR and VR use on developing brains. Nonetheless, one thing is clear, the future is bright for augmented and virtual reality, and the disabled can benefit immensely from it.[8] There is so much to look forward to in this area of technology.

XR Access

XR Access is a community dedicated to making augmented and virtual reality accessible to people with all abilities. In July of 2019, the first ever XR Access event was held at Cornell Tech on Randall's Island in New York

---

[8]Augmented Virtual Reality benefit Disabled People `www.thegenius.ca/augmented-virtual-reality-benefit-disabled-people/`

(Figure 10-5). The purpose of the event was to bring together industry professionals, educators, and mixed reality experts to discuss the future of extended realities, otherwise known as XR (virtual reality, augmented reality, and mixed reality) and accessibility.

Figure 10-5. *XR Access Event audience at Cornell Tech in 2019. Photo by Christopher Farber*

Unlike the Web, there are no set guidelines yet related to XR and accessibility. As an attendee at the event, I was able to listen to five different talks and participate in breakout discussions about what it might take to make more accessible. Here are excerpts from those talks.

Talk 1: XR Access, What Does It Mean?

Richard Ladner, University of Washington

Prof. Ladner began by defining accessibility and inclusive design and posing critical questions for the XR Access movement. Accessible products and services are those that can be used by anyone, including those with disabilities. Accessible products and services use accessible infrastructure across different products and services, such as optical character recognition, technology that converts an image of text to text, speech recognition, and text-to-speech. He concluded with three questions to set the foundation for the day's work:

1. What should the XR access infrastructure be?

2. How do you get designers and developers to use the infrastructure to create accessible design experiences?

3. What policies and industry incentives are needed to make XR accessible in the future?

Talk 2: XR and Accessibility

Steven Feiner, Columbia University

Prof. Feiner presented an overview of XR technologies, from pioneering XR prototypes developed in the 1960s through today's technology and its promise for the future. He began by defining XR, which represents a variety of terms used to describe a range of experiences: augmented reality, virtual reality, artificial reality, mediated reality, etc. Regardless of the term, XR refers to an interactive 3D world of media that is generated and tracked relative to the user. Prof. Feiner described the three main kinds of XR systems: optical see-through, video see-through, and projection. As seen through these categories, XR creators have been focused on the visual aspects of the experience. Prof. Feiner described XR experiences from an audio-focused perspective. For example, an aural hear-through display, as opposed to an optical see-through display, is one that plays virtual 3D sounds without obstructing the user's hearing. Prof. Feiner concluded by describing several of his lab's research projects, showing the range of possible XR applications.

Talk 3: SeeingVR, A Set of Tools to Make Virtual Reality More Accessible to People with Low Vision

Yuhang Zhao, Cornell Tech, Cornell University

SeeingVR, developed in collaboration with Microsoft Research, offers a set of tools to make VR applications more accessible to people with low vision. They include a magnifying lens, brightness enhancement, and edge overlays that make a scene more visible. Most of the tools can be applied to an existing application by the user, without requiring the developer to make any changes to the code. SeeingVR is open source, and the code can be accessed at `https://github.com/microsoft/SeeingVRtoolkit`

Talk 4: Living in an Augmented World

Chancey Fleet, New York Public Library

Fleet described her experiences with (in)accessible products, delineated why change is critical, and envisioned a world of XR technologies that are born accessible. Fleet has been told repeatedly by designers and developers that "making products accessible was not the focus of their work," "not a current priority," or "not within scope." But she argued, accessibility matters, as XR technology designed with accessibility in mind can lead to innovations for everyone. For Fleet, reality is already augmented. For example, she relies on applications on her phone to navigate by receiving descriptions of nearby objects and landmarks. She expressed her hope that our imaginations will help lead this journey for both practical ends and for fun and creativity. She closed with her wish, "to sit on a virtual chair and hear the sounds of virtual birds."

Talk 5: Movers and Shakers

Glenn Cantave, Movers and Shakers/NYC

Cantave is an activist, performance artist, and social entrepreneur who uses XR to highlight narratives of the oppressed (Figure 10-6). He explained his work illustrating how history is traditionally told from the perspectives of those in power. For example, nearly all monuments in New York City represent white men. Movers and Shakers/NYC seeks to empower oppressed communities—African-American descendants of slaves in particular—through augmented reality experiences while also closing the digital divide for youth from disadvantaged backgrounds. Among their projects, Cantave described how Movers and Shakers has collaborated with New York City schools to create rooms where students can learn from virtual historical figures from oppressed populations. In parallel to his work, he reflected on the importance of giving people with disabilities a voice and a role in the technology creation process to ensure that XR access is a priority.[9]

---

[9]XR Access Report compiled by Shiri Azenkot, Larry Goldberg, Jessie Taft, and Sam Soloway based on notes and presentations from the XR Access Symposium

Figure 10-6. *Glenn Cantave of Movers and Shakers gives his plenary talk at the XR Access Symposium (photo by Christopher Farber)*

After the talks, we broke out into groups and started out with more questions than answers. Based off of prompts from a moderator, we were able to address various aspects of the experiences such as authoring tools, content and creative, definitions and measurements, devices and platforms, education, frameworks for the future, image and video, input modalities, mobility, sensation and cognition, sound and haptic technologies, and standards and policies. XR Access was a great event that provided a platform to discuss the issues related to creating more accessible experiences. If XR is the future, it is up to us to ensure that it's an experience for people of all abilities.

Artificial Intelligence and Accessibility

Another technology moving accessibility forward is artificial intelligence (AI). AI is a system of computers that can perform tasks similar to a human. AI can see, hear, translate, and make decisions. An example of AI being used for accessibility today is the Microsoft application "Seeing AI," which allows people with visual disability to complete multiple tasks with one application, and it is powered by AI. Figure 10-7 shows the Microsoft web site showing Seeing AI, A free app that narrates the world around you. Designed for the low-vision community, this research project harnesses the power of AI to describe people, text, and objects.

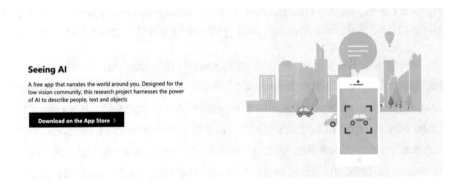

Figure 10-7. Seeing AI download page on the Microsoft web site

Table 10-1 lists some of the things that Seeing AI can do.[10]

Table 10-1. *Seeing AI capabilities*

Capability	Description
Short Texts	Speak to text as soon as it appears on the screen
Documents	Provides audio guidance to capture a printed page and recognizes text, along with its original formatting
Products	Gives audio beeps to help locate barcodes and then scans them to identify products
Person	Recognizes friends and describes people around you, including their emotions
Scene	An experimental feature to describe the scene around you
Currency	Identify currency bills when paying with cash
Light	Generate an audible tone corresponding to the brightness in your surroundings
Color	Describe perceived color
Handwriting	Reads handwritten text

Where might AI take us in the future? In addition to Microsoft, Google is also working on using artificial intelligence related to accessibility with products such as Lookout which works similar to Seeing AI and narrates the environment in real time.

---

[10]Seeing AI www.microsoft.com/en-us/ai/seeing-ai

LIVE CAPTIONING

I got to facilitate a Service Design meetup in NYC. Before the event, I received a text from a friend who is deaf. Her battery died for her hearing aid and she requested that I use Google Slides because Google Slides gives people the ability to use Live Captions (Live Captions is powered by AI). Originally, I had created my slides for the presentation in Keynote and quickly had to change to update to Google Slides.

Ultimately, my friend did not show up for the event, but I did end up using Live Captions and the audience benefited from it, because many of them did not know it existed, and people were able to see Live Captioning, and they were able to see that the captioning only worked when I was close to my computer. The following screens show the text exchange between my friend and me. My friend's hearing battery died and she requested my slides use Live Text.

Hey Regine, can you make sure your presentation today has Google captioning?

My hearing battery just died, I forgot to bring a spare, and they don't sell the battery in stores-- honestly this is the reason I'm putting this hackathon event together. But would love to listen (read, really) to what you have to say!

Hey '

I will do my best. I originally had it in Keynote.

Let me see what I can do

I can just watch the recording!

Tue, Aug 13, 17:53

Hey Regine, heading out of the office. Should I go or check out the recording?

It was an important lesson for me, and had me rethink future presentations moving forward. At the time, I wasn't thinking about artificial intelligence, I was just thinking I need to make this the most accessible experience it can be in order not to leave anyone out. Creating inclusive experiences takes constant awareness and flexibility.

You Try It: Bonus Exercise

In this exercise, we'll present slides with captions. Go to Google Slides `https://www.google.com/slides/about/` (Figure 10-8).

You can turn on automatic captions to display the speaker's words in real time at the bottom of the screen. This feature is available in US English only, using Chrome on a computer.

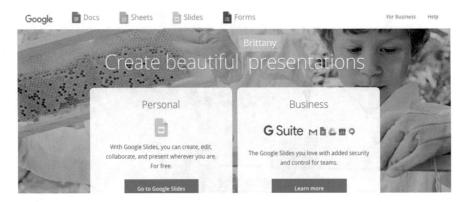

Figure 10-8. *Google Slides landing page*

Step 1: Set Up Your Microphone

1. To use captions with Google Slides, your computer microphone needs to be on and working.

2. Devices and microphones vary, so check your computer manual for instructions. Microphone settings are typically in the System Preferences on a Mac or the Control Panel on a PC.

3. Google Slides uses the computer's microphone or an external microphone paired with the computer (such as a handheld microphone).

Step 2: Present with Captions

1. Make sure that you have a working Internet connection.

2. On your computer, open your presentation in Google Slides.

3. To start presenting, click Present or press the shortcut for your browser:

    Chrome OS: Ctrl + Search + 5

    Windows: Ctrl + F5

    Mac: ⌘ + Shift + Enter

4. To turn on captions, click CC or press the shortcut for your browser:

    Chrome OS or Windows: Ctrl + Shift + c

    Mac: ⌘ + Shift + c

5. As you speak, captions appear at the bottom of the screen. Captions don't include punctuation.

6. To turn off captions, click CC or press the shortcut for your browser:

    Chrome OS or Windows: Ctrl + Shift + c

    Mac: ⌘ + Shift + c

Note   Captions are not stored.

Tips for Using Captions

If you present slides over video conferencing software (such as Hangouts Meet), captions show up on the shared screen. To set expectations for your audience, it's a good idea to tell them that captions are from Google Slides, not the video conferencing software, and that only the speaker's voice is captioned.

Some people find captions distracting, so you might want to ask your audience before turning on captions.

Captions and your microphone automatically turn off if there's no activity on your computer for 30 minutes.

Troubleshooting Captions

If captions aren't working, try these tips:

> If possible, reduce background noise or move to a quieter room.
>
> In your system and browser preferences, check your microphone settings.
>
> Plug in an external microphone, if you haven't already.
>
> Check that your microphone is plugged in and isn't being used by another application.
>
> Change the input volume on your microphone.
>
> Restart your computer.
>
> Clear your browser's cache.

Note   Caption text is powered by machine learning and depends on audio input from the speaker, including the speaker's accent, voice modulation, and intonation. As language understanding models use billions of common phrases and sentences to automatically transcribe spoken words, they can also reflect human cognitive biases. As such, captions might not be a complete and accurate transcription of the speaker's words.

Conclusion

Past and present innovations show us that there are endless opportunities when it comes to making a more inclusive world. When it comes to innovation, we all could be a little more WOQE:

Watch. Be awake!

Observe. Check out your surroundings—if you had a disability, would you be able to use the entrance you just came through? Would you be able to use the web site you were just on, using a keyboard?

Question. Question everything. If things are not accessible or inclusive, question why.

Explore. Familiarize yourself with perspectives other than your own.

The illiterate of the 21st century will not be those who cannot read and write, but those who cannot learn, unlearn, and relearn.

—Alvin Toffler

This is the end of the book, but not the end of the opportunity to go and make more inclusive products. Not only do you have the opportunity to design for others, you can also make things better for yourself. When we create more accessible and inclusive experiences, we are allowing others to experience things and not exclude them. We all know what it feels like to be left out. Let's make a more inclusive world. Never stop learning and never stop growing.

APPENDIX A

Accessible Heuristics

ACCESSIBILITY HEURISTICS, V1.4

10 General Rules of thumb for Accessible Design[1]

Table A-1.

INTERACTION METHODS AND MODALITIES	Users can efficiently interact with the system using the input method of their choosing (i.e., mouse, keyboard, touch, etc.).
NAVIGATION AND WAYFINDING	Users can easily navigate, find content, and determine where they are at all times within the system.
STRUCTURE AND SEMANTICS	Users can make sense of the structure of the content on each page and understand how to operate within the system.

(continued)

---

[1]Accessibility Heuristics Denis Boudreau, Aparna Pasi, Caitlin Geaier https://www.24a11y.com/2018/unlocking-accessibility-for-ux-ui-designers/ - https://drive.google.com/file/d/1QkURByXUk4NOtl7jw6VtyCUi4_JjlP6d/edit

Table A-1. (*continued*)

ERROR PREVENTION AND STATES	Interactive controls have persistent, meaningful instructions to help prevent mistakes and provide users with clear error states which indicate what the problems are and how to fix them whenever errors are returned.
CONTRAST AND LEGIBILITY	Text and other meaningful information can be easily distinguished and read by users of the system.
LANGUAGE AND READABILITY	Content on the page can easily be read and understood by users of the system.
PREDICTABILITY AND CONSISTENCY	The purpose of each element is predictable, and how each element relates to the system as a whole is clear and meaningful, to avoid confusion for the users.
TIMING AND PRESERVATION	Users are given enough time to complete their tasks and do not lose information if their time (i.e., a session) runs out.
MOVEMENT AND FLASHING	Elements on the page that move, flash, or animate in other ways can be stopped, and do not distract or harm the users.
VISUAL AND AUDITORY ALTERNATIVES	Purely visual or auditory content that conveys information has text-based alternatives for users who can't see or hear.

A11Y Style Guide[2]

Table A-2.

Basic Card	• Make sure you have tabbing focus indicators for all elements that need to be highlighted.
	• Every `<img>` you add to your site needs to have an alt attribute. If the image is informational, set the `alt` equal to a *descriptive* alternative for that image.
	• If the image is decorative or redundant to adjacent text, set `alt=""`, which conveys to assistive technology users that the image isn't necessary for understanding the page.
	• Avoid using generic strings like photo, image, or icon as `alt` values, as they don't communicate valuable content to the user. Be as descriptive as possible. You can add `class="visuallyhidden"` with descriptive text to give more context to a button or link's purpose.

(continued)

---

[2]A11Y Style Guide `https://a11y-style-guide.com/style-guide/`

Table A-2. (*continued*)

Forms— Checkboxes	• The `<fieldset>` surrounds the entire grouping of checkboxes or radio buttons. The `<legend>` provides a description for the grouping. • Some assistive technology reads the legend text for each fieldset, so it should be brief and descriptive. This helps someone using assistive technology to understand the question they are answering with the group of checkboxes. • WAI-ARIA provides a grouping role that functions similarly to `fieldset` and `legend`. In option #2 the `div` element has `role=group` to indicate that the contained elements are members of a group and the `aria-labelledby` attribute references the id for text that will serve as the label for the group. **Note:** This method is not supported by all browser/AT devices.
Buttons	• A `<button>` tag does not need anything special to work. Use `<button>` when you can, but it is possible to use other elements as long as you add `role="button"` and add JavaScript to replicate the button functionality. • Just like links, you can add `class="visuallyhidden"` with descriptive text to give more context to the button's purpose. • If a button contains an `<img>` element, make sure to set its `alt` attribute. If it contains an icon, use `aria-label` to describe the icon instead. • You can use `<input type="image">` to make a graphical button. It takes a `src` and `alt` attribute just like traditional images. • Button states are important, not just button styling! If you are only toggling classes to visually manage state of your components, you are likely not appropriately conveying that state to users of assistive technologies.

(*continued*)

Table A-2. (*continued*)

Colors	• Avoid using color *only* to communicate information. In the case of links, use another identifier such as bold or underline to indicate a link vs. using color alone.
	• Some users have difficulty reading text if there is too little contrast between foreground and background. To meet Level AA, text must have a contrast ratio of at least 4.5:1 (or 3:1 for large text). In order to meet the guidelines at the stricter Level AAA, the contrast ratio must be at least 7:1 (or 4.5:1 for large text).
Link Focus	• Do not set your site's link focus to outline: none. Never. Ever.
	• If you have multiple form fields on your site or you see the dreaded outline: none in your base code, you can reset the browser defaults by adding the code:

```
a:focus {
    outline: auto 2px Highlight; // for non-
    webkit browsers
    outline: auto 5px -webkit-focus-ring-color;
    // for webkit browsers
}
```

• Of course, you can create your own focus styles to match your theme or to make the default browser styles more prominent, just make sure they are visible by tabbing and obvious to your users.

(*continued*)

Table A-2. (*continued*)

Read More Links	• Add id selectors to titles or paragraphs and use `aria-labelledby=""` to link to the title text (Example #1).
	• Add descriptive text with `aria-label=""` directly in the link (Example #2).
	• Add id selectors to titles or paragraphs and use `aria-describedby=""` to link to the title text (Example #3).
	• Use the class `visuallyhidden` to visually hide more information about the link (Example #4).
	• Turn read more links into buttons, when you can, since they allow for more labeling options.
Skip Links	• Provide ways for users to skip to important sections of your website. This will help users using screen readers navigate your site easier and more efficiently.
	• There is no real theming rule when it comes to styling your skip links, as such a lot of websites tend to hide them with `class="visuallyhidden"` with a special focus attribute so that sighted keyboard only users are able to see them.
	• It is important to see that the link points to a valid HTML ID, as often this is overlooked in implementation.
	• On the a11y Style Guide site we have used 'Jump to main content', but other valid examples of "skip" links include:

(*continued*)

Table A-2. (*continued*)

Typography	• Avoid small font sizes.
	• Use relative units for font size, such as ems or rems. While modern browsers can smoothly zoom pixel-based layouts, sizing type in relative units ensures an entire layout can be scaled up or down by simply updating the font size of the body element.
	• A design should allow typography to be magnified up to 200% by the user without clipping or distorting content.
	• Select basic, simple, easily readable fonts and use a limited number of fonts.
	• Avoid small font sizes and use relative units for font size (ems or rems).
	• Limit the use of font variations such as bold, italics, and ALL CAPITAL LETTERS (caps are similar to screaming to screen readers).
	• Don't rely only on the appearance of the font (color, shape, font variation, placement, etc.) to convey meaning.
	• Avoid blinking or moving text.
	• Use real text rather than text within graphics.
Audio	• Build your media with accessibility in mind! It is much easier to work accessibility into the beginning than trying to tack it on later. This is true of all components, but especially for media components.
	• Make sure your player is accessible and includes control elements to pause, stop, and play your media.
	• Do not auto-play your media. This can cause confusion as well as annoyance.
	• Make sure your media has alternative methods to get to the content. For example, add transcripts of your audio files.

(*continued*)

Table A-2. (*continued*)

Image Gallery	• Every `<img>` you add to your site needs to have an alt attribute. If the image is informational, set the `alt` equal to a *descriptive* alternative for that image.
	• Avoid using generic strings like photo, image, or icon as `alt` values, as they don't communicate valuable content to the user. Be as descriptive as possible.
Images	• Every `<img>` you add to your site needs to have an alt attribute. If the image is informational, set the `alt` equal to a *descriptive* alternative for that image.
	• If the image is decorative or redundant to adjacent text, set `alt=""`, which conveys to assistive technology users that the image isn't necessary for understanding the page.
	• Avoid using generic strings like photo, image, or icon as `alt` values, as they don't communicate valuable content to the user. Be as descriptive as possible.
	• Make sure any text in images of text is at least 14 points and has good contrast with the background.
Site Logo	• Every `<img>` you add to your site needs to have an alt attribute. If the image is informational, set the `alt` equal to a *descriptive* alternative for that image.
	• Avoid using generic strings like photo, image, or icon as `alt` values, as they don't communicate valuable content to the user. Be as descriptive as possible.
	• Make sure any text in images of text is at least 14 points and has good contrast with the background.
	• When using images as links, one must consider how the `alt` text will be read back to users of assistive technology. The following examples showcase appropriate `alt` text for logos when used as a link, or as a stand-alone image asset.

(*continued*)

Table A-2. (*continued*)

SVG's	• SVGs are scalable vector graphics and can be made used for icons, images, logos, etc. SVG content is scalable and scales without any reduction in visual quality.
	• The best way to make SVGs accessible to assistive technologies (AT) like screen readers and speech recognition tools is to put it directly into your HTML using the `<svg>` tag
	• Avoid using `<embed>`, `<object>`, or `<img>` elements as they are not as supported by browsers as inline SVG
	• Include a `<title>` and `<description>` in your SVG markup
	• Use `aria-labelledby=""` and reference the id values of the title and description elements
	• Give your SVGs a job with the `role=""` attribute
	• To "hide" elements from a screen reader in an SVG add `role="presentation"`
Videos	• Build your media with accessibility in mind! It is much easier to work accessibility into the beginning than trying to tack it on later. This is true of all components, but especially for media components.
	• Make sure your player is accessible and includes control elements to pause, stop, and play your media.
	• Do not auto-play your media. This can cause confusion as well as annoyance.
	• Make sure your media has alternative methods to get to the content. For example, add captions to your videos and/or provide a transcript for your users to read.
	• Make sure your media does not cause seizures! Use the Photosensitive Epilepsy Analysis Tool (PEAT) to check your media before you add it to your web site.

(*continued*)

Table A-2. *(continued)*

Navigation—Accordion	• Buttons are used as the accordions so that they are tab-able by keyboard users and accessible to screen readers. • Each accordion button and related content has a unique `id` associated with its `aria-controls`. • Each button has an `aria-expanded` attribute on it that is toggled between true and false. If `aria-expanded='true'`, the content associated with it is shown, and if `aria-expanded='false'` the content is hidden.
Breadcrumbs	• Place the breadcrumb in a `<nav>` element when you can. • If you do not use a `<nav>` element, you need to add `role="navigation"` to the markup. **Note:** this role is implied when you use the `<nav>` element, so it is a bit redundant to use both at the same time. • The markup includes an `aria-label="breadcrumbs"` to describe the type of navigation. • Add `aria-current="page"` to the link that points to the current page. This will tell assistive technology (AT) devices that the focused link is pointing to the current page.
Basic Navigation	• All navigation elements should have a `<nav>` tag. • If you have to use a more generic element such as a `<div>`, add `role="navigation"` to every navbar to explicitly identify it as a landmark region for users of assistive technologies. • Menus should be labeled according to their individual function. You can use `class="visuallyhidden">`, `aria-label=""`, or `aria-labelledby=""` to easily add context to the different menus on your site.

(continued)

Table A-2. (*continued*)

Dropdown Navigation	• All navigation elements should have a `<nav>` tag. • If you have to use a more generic element such as a `<div>`, add `role="navigation"` to every navbar to explicitly identify it as a landmark region for users of assistive technologies. • Menus should be labeled according to their individual function. You can use `class="visuallyhidden">`, `aria-label=""`, or `aria-labelledby=""` to easily add context to the different menus on your site.
Footer Navigation	• All navigation elements should have a `<nav>` tag. • If you have to use a more generic element such as a `<div>`, add `role="navigation"` to every navbar to explicitly identify it as a landmark region for users of assistive technologies. • Menus should be labeled according to their individual function. You can use `class="visuallyhidden">`, `aria-label=""`, or `aria-labelledby=""` to easily add context to the different menus on your site.
Mobile Navigation	• Use the `<button>` element for your mobile navigation icon. • If you use an icon that is purely decoration, declare `alt=""`, as no additional information is needed. If the icon you are using *is* important to the functionality, then supply additional `alt="_descriptive text goes here_"` information. • It is helpful to all users when you add descriptive text when displaying a mobile icon to give more context to the button's purpose. • Place mobile open/close buttons within the `<nav>` element and use them to toggle state of another child wrapper of the nav. This will ensure that the navigation landmark is still discoverable by screen readers, even if it is in a closed/hidden state.

(*continued*)

Table A-2. (*continued*)

Pagination	<ul><li>Place the pager in a `<nav>` element when you can.</li><li>If you do not use a `<nav>` element, you need to add `role="navigation"` to the markup. **Note:** this role is implied when you use the `<nav>` element so it is a bit redundant to use both at the same time.</li><li>The markup includes an `aria-label="pagination"` to describe the type of navigation.</li><li>Add `aria-current="page"` to the link that points to the current page. This will tell AT that the focused link is pointing to the current page.</li><li>Add `aria-disabled="true"` to the link when the link is disabled.</li></ul>
Headings	<ul><li>Navigating through the `<h1>` and `<h2>` give a user an overview of a page and how its content is structured. The `<h3>` through `<h6>` elements provide a quick understanding of the details in each section.</li><li>Heading tags should be in order. That means an `<h1>` is followed by an `<h2>`, an `<h2>` is followed by a `<h2>` or `<h3>`, and so on. It *is* okay to skip heading levels when going up in order (ex. `<h4>` to `<h1>`).</li><li>Keep heading tags consistent. Inconsistently implementing headings can create confusion and frustration for users using assistive technologies.</li><li>Do not style text to give the visual appearance of headings—use actual heading tags.</li></ul>

(*continued*)

Table A-2. (*continued*)

Lists	• Creating accessible lists is fairly straightforward and easy *if* you use the correct markup.
	• Use ol markup to group ordered lists; use ul markup to group unordered lists; and use dl markup to group terms with their definitions.
	• Simple comma-separated lists may not need list markup, but longer lists or groups of links should have it.
Tables	• Tables with one header and simple data are fairly accessible out of the box and may not need additional accessibility updates. Always use the simplest table configuration possible.
	• When your tables get more complex, use the `<th>` element to identify the header cells by adding a scope attribute. For header rows use `<th scope="row">`. For header columns use `<th scope="col">`
	• Add the optional `<caption>` element before the table content to give users more information on the table contents. Think of it as a headline for your table.
Tabs - Draft	• Be mindful of using tabs, as they are less discoverable by design.
	• Once a tab button is focused, other tabs can be selected with the arrow keys.
	• A tab's contents can be accessed via Tab (if there are focusable elements in the tab well) or PgDn (if there are no focusable elements in the tab well).
	• Be sure to update the values of the `aria-posinset` and `aria-setsize` attributes if you have more than three tabs.

Periodic Table of Semantics by Gerard Cohen

Periodic Table of Semantics by Gerard Cohen `https://gerardkcohen.github.io/periodic-table-of-semantics.html`

Assistive Technologies and Adaptive Strategies

From the IAAP (International Association of Accessibilty Professionals) Study Guide—ICT stands for Information and Communication Technology

Color Blindness: Examples of Assistive Technologies and Adaptive Strategies

Domain	Challenges	Solutions
General	Certain color combinations—red and green in particular—can be difficult to distinguish	Materials can be designed in a way that does not depend on color as a way to convey information.

Reading Disabilities and ICT: Examples of Assistive Technologies and Adaptive Strategies

Domain	Challenges	Solutions
ICT	Often perceive words as floating and not in a line	Can use a special font developed for dyslexia which weights the letters down and makes similar figures appear differently May be granted additional time to complete tasks
ICT	Often perceive words differently than others such as seeing p b d q as the same letter	Can use a special font developed for dyslexia which weights the letters down and makes similar figures appear differently May be granted additional time to complete tasks
ICT	Often require additional time to read and process content	Can extend time-outs and return to the same location on the page Can use a screen reader to get content in an auditory method to reinforce what is being seen Can use screen readers which highlight the word or phrase being read to assist with tracking Can use enhanced visible focus indicators to keep track of their position on the page Can use special programs or dictionaries which present words with pictures May be granted additional time to complete tasks

(continued)

233

Domain	Challenges	Solutions
ICT	Often have the burden of deciphering content from the way it is presented	May apply a custom style sheet
ICT	May have difficulty solving problems presented through security features such as CAPTCHA	Ability to change the type of problem presented
ICT	May have difficulty processing content through visual means	Can use a screen reader to get content in an auditory method to reinforce what is being seen May be granted additional time to complete tasks
ICT	May have a hard time spelling words correctly	Can use a spelling and grammar checker

Blindness: Examples of Assistive Technologies and Adaptive Strategies

Domain	Challenges	Solutions
ICT	Cannot see digital or electronic interfaces (computers, automated teller machines (ATMs), mobile devices, airport kiosks, televisions, printers, copiers, phones, GPS devices, etc.)	Screen readers can read interfaces and content out loud to users by converting digital text to synthesized speech, but only if they have been designed to be accessible. Self-voicing interfaces and applications can communicate to users without the need for a screen reader, but these are appropriate mostly for broadcasting information, because they usually do not use or interact with the interface or content as screen readers do. Refreshable braille output devices use screen readers to convert digital text to braille. These devices are typically expensive, and only a minority of blind people know how to read Braille.
ICT	Cannot use screen readers on digital content and interfaces not designed with accessibility in mind	Interface designers and content authors can edit the markup to make it compatible with the assistive technologies used by blind people.

(continued)

Domain	Challenges	Solutions
Architecture and Built Environment	Cannot see when walking	Can help blind people feel their surroundings as they walk. Service animals (e.g., "Seeing Eye" dogs), trained to assist blind people, help them navigate their surroundings. GPS-based walking instructions with an audio interface, either automated or via a remote human navigator. Raised tiles on the ground to indicate the edge of a platform, a pathway along a sidewalk, the beginning of a staircase, etc. Eliminate low-hanging architectural features that a blind person could bump into. Clear pathways without obstructions in hallways, sidewalks.
Architecture and Built Environment	Cannot see signs or other text on buildings or other areas in the built environment	Map and geolocation applications on mobile devices can announce the names and descriptions of buildings and other location-related information. Braille labels and descriptions on entrances, rooms, bathrooms, historical markers, and other points of interest can allow blind people to explore and understand their surroundings, as long as the person knows braille, and as long as the braille labels are easy to find. Tactile models of the exterior of buildings or of floorplans of the interior of buildings help blind people form a mental map of their surroundings.

Domain	Challenges	Solutions
Consumer and Industrial Products	Cannot see or feel the controls on flat interfaces on consumer devices such as microwaves, ovens, dishwashers, etc.	Alternative interfaces with knobs or other tactile controls. Audio interfaces. Remote control through applications on mobile devices.
Consumer and Industrial Products	Cannot read the text on the containers or packaging for consumer items such as medicine, toothpaste, shampoo, sunscreen, hand cream, personal care products, foods, drinks, and candy	Embossed braille (or braille stickers) on packaging and product containers help consumers identify items both in the store and after purchase.

(continued)

Domain	Challenges	Solutions
Consumer and Industrial Products	Cannot read money to determine its value	Applications on mobile devices can photograph the money and read the value to blind people. Paper bills and coins could be manufactured in different sizes, shapes, or textures to allow blind people to distinguish the value based on touch. Non-cache systems of payment can allow blind people to make financial transactions via computers, mobile devices, or on-site payment hardware with screen readers or self-voicing output.
Consumer and Industrial Products	Cannot read books, magazines, posters, postal mail, or other printed materials	Optical character recognition software can convert scanned images of text into digital text readable by screen readers. The accuracy of the conversion depends on the quality of the original document, as well as font choices, line spacing, and the quality of the conversion software itself. Information can be placed online or in other digital formats to allow blind people to read the materials using their own assistive technologies.

Low Vision: Examples of Assistive Technologies and Adaptive Strategies

Domain	Challenges	Solutions
General	Small text can be hard to read.	Screen magnifiers can enlarge the items on the screen to make them easier to read.
		Utilities to enhance contrast, change colors, or alter other aspects of visual appearance can improve legibility.
		Screen readers can supplement screen magnifiers by reading interfaces and content out loud to users through synthesized speech, but only if the digital information has been designed to be accessible. Self-voicing interfaces (on ATMs, kiosks, transportation systems, etc.) and applications can communicate to users without the need for a screen reader, but these are appropriate mostly for broadcasting information, because they usually do not use or interact with the interface or content as screen readers do.
		Alternative large print versions of small print text can make printed materials easier to read.
		Alternative digital versions (web, mobile applications, etc.) of printed materials can give users the ability to read the materials using their own assistive technologies.
General	Low-contrast text can be hard to read.	Software or hardware options can enhance the contrast of digital text. Interface designers and content creators can choose color combinations with high-enough contrast to easily read.

Math and ICT: Examples of Assistive Technologies and Adaptive Strategies

Domain	Challenges	Solutions
ICT	Inability to distinguish right from left in graphic images	Can read data in a data table or text description as an alternative to graphic representations of data when an alternative is provided May be granted additional time to complete tasks
ICT	Inability to copy graphs, figures, and diagrams	Can use speech-to-text to verbalize instructions for completing homework and test questions when the questions are designed to accessibility guidelines and text-to-speech assistive technology can access content May be granted additional time to complete tasks
ICT	Inability to perform calculations	Can use an accessibility accommodation link to a reference sheet with common equations when provided Can use an onscreen calculator as an accommodation May be granted additional time to complete tasks

Speech and Language: Examples of Assistive Technologies and Adaptive Strategies[3]

Domain	Challenges	Solutions
ICT	Often require repeated exposure to content before long-term memory processing and comprehension takes place	Screen readers can read interfaces and content out loud to users by converting digital text to synthesized speech, but only if they have been designed to be accessible. Users can adjust rate of speech; vary voice and pitch for repeated yet varied exposure to content. May be granted additional time to complete tasks
ICT	Cannot use screen readers on digital content and interfaces not designed with accessibility in mind	Interface designers and content authors can edit the markup to make it compatible with the assistive technologies used by those with speech and language disabilities May be granted additional time to complete tasks
ICT	May have difficulty writing understandable text	May use programs with writing templates, organizational tools, word prediction, and spell checkers May use speech-to-text programs May be granted additional time to complete tasks

[3]IAAP Exam Prep IAAP CPACC BOK 2017_062317
https://www.accessibilityassociation.org/exampreparation

WCAG 2 for Designers[4]

Success Criteria	Area of focus
1.3.1 Info and Relationships (A) (2.0)	• Organize pages using properly nested HTML headings. • Use ARIA landmarks and labels to identify regions of a page. • Reserve tables for tabular data, use table headers appropriately, and use table captions.
1.3.4 Orientation (AA) (2.1)	• All content and functionality should be available regardless of whether a mobile device is oriented vertically or horizontally, unless the orientation of the device is absolutely essential.
1.4.1 Use of Color (A) (2.0)	• When the color of words, backgrounds, or other content is used to convey information, also include the information in text. • Links should always be easily identifiable through noncolor means, including both default and hover states. The easiest and most conventional way to signify links is underlining. • Required fields and fields with errors must include some noncolor ways to identify them.
1.4.2 Audio Control (A) (2.0)	• Do not have audio that plays automatically on the page. When providing audio, also provide an easy way to disable the audio and adjust the volume.

---

[4]WCAG 2 Checklist for designers https://usability.yale.edu/
web-accessibility/articles/wcag2-checklist/designers

Success Criteria	Area of focus
1.4.3 Contrast (Minimum) (AA) (2.0)	• Text (including images of text) have a contrast ratio of at least 4.5:1. For text and images of at least 24px and normal weight or 19px and bold, use a contrast ratio that is at least 3:1.
1.4.5 Images of Text (AA) (2.0)	• Avoid images of text, except in cases such as logos.
1.4.10 Reflow (AA) (2.1)	• Provide responsive style sheets such that content can be displayed at 320px wide without horizontal scrolling. (Content which must be displayed in two dimensions, such as maps and data tables, may have horizontal scrolling.)
1.4.11 Non-text Contrast (AA) (2.1)	• Color contrast for graphics and interactive UI components must be at least 3:1 so that different parts can be distinguished. • When providing custom states for elements (e.g., hover, active, focus), color contrast for those states should be at least 3:1.
1.4.13 Content on Hover or Focus (AA) (2.1)	• For content that appears on hover and focus: the content should be dismissible with the escape key; the content itself can be hovered over; and the content remains available unless it is dismissed, it is no longer relevant, or the user removes hover and focus. • To the extent possible, content that appears on hover or focus should not obscure other content, unless it presents a form input error or can be dismissed with the escape key.

(continued)

243

Success Criteria	Area of focus
2.1.1 Keyboard (A) (2.0)	• All functionality should be available to a keyboard without requiring specific timing of keystrokes, unless the functionality cannot be provided by a keyboard alone.
2.2.2 Pause, Stop, Hide (A) (2.0)	• Items on the page should not automatically move, blink, scroll, or update, including carousels. If content does automatically move, blink, scroll, or update, provide a way to pause, stop, or hide the moving, blinking, scrolling, or updating.
2.3.1 Three Flashes or Below Threshold (A) (2.0)	• Do not provide any content that flashes more than three times in any 1-second period.
2.4.3 Focus Order (A) (2.0)	• Create a logical tab order through links, form controls, and interactive objects. • When inserting content into the DOM, insert the content immediately after the triggering element, or use scripting to manage focus in an intuitive way. When triggering dialogs and menus, make sure those elements follow their trigger in the focus order in an intuitive way. When content is dismissed or removed, place focus back on the trigger.
2.4.4 Link Purpose (In Context) (A) (2.0)	• The purpose of each link can be determined from the link text alone, or from the link text and the containing paragraph, list item, or table cell, or the link text and the title attribute.
2.4.5 Multiple Ways (AA) (2.0)	• Each web site should include at least two of the following: a list of related pages; table of contents; site map; search; or list of all pages.

Success Criteria	Area of focus
2.4.6 Headings and Labels (AA) (2.0)	• Ensure that on each page, headings, landmark labels, and form labels are unique unless the structure provides adequate differentiation between them.
2.4.7 Focus Visible (AA) (2.0)(link is external)	• Provide keyboard focus styles that are highly visible, and make sure that a visible element has focus at all times when using a keyboard. Do not rely on browser default focus styles.
2.5.1 Pointer Gestures (A) (2.1)	• Do not require multipoint or path-based gestures (e.g., pinching, swiping, dragging) for functionality unless the gesture is essential to the functionality.
2.5.2 Pointer Cancellation (A) (2.1)	• Avoid triggering functionality on down-events, such as onmousedown. Use events such as onclick instead. • If a function is triggered on an up-event (e.g., onmouseup), provide a way to abort or undo the function.
2.5.4 Motion Actuation (A) (2.1)	• Avoid activating functionality through motion (e.g., shaking a phone). If motion triggers functionality, provide a way to disable the motion trigger, and provide an alternative way to activate the functionality.
3.2.1 On Focus (A) (2.0)	• When the focus changes, the page should not cause a change in page content, spawn a new browser window, submit a form, cause further change in focus, or cause any other change that disorients the user.

(continued)

Success Criteria	Area of focus
3.2.2 On Input (A) (2.0)	• When a user inputs information or interacts with a control, the page should not cause a change in page content, spawn a new browser window, submit a form, cause further change in focus, or cause any other change that disorients the user. If an input causes such a change, the user must be informed ahead of time.
3.2.3 Consistent Navigation (AA) (2.0)	• When components are repeated across web page, they should appear in the same relative order with regard to other repeated components on each web page where they appear. • When a navigation menu is presented on multiple pages, the links should appear in the same order on each page.
3.2.4 Consistent Identification (AA) (2.0) **3.3.1 Error Identification (A) (2.0)**	• When components have the same functionality across several web pages, the components are labeled consistently on each page • Programmatically indicate required fields using the required or aria-required att • Programmatically indicate required fields using the required or aria-required attributes. Also, visually indicate required fields in the form's instructions or form labels. Do not indicate required fields for CSS alone. • Make errors easy to discover, identify, and correct.

Success Criteria	Area of focus
3.3.2 Labels or Instructions (A) (2.0)	• Use semantic, descriptive labels for inputs. Visually position labels in a consistent way that makes associating labels with form controls easy. Do not rely on placeholder text in lieu of an HTML label. • Provide text instructions at the beginning of a form or set of fields that describes the necessary input.
3.3.3 Error Suggestion (AA) (2.0)	• If an input error is detected and if suggestions for correction are known, provide suggestions for fixing the submission.
3.3.4 Error Prevention (Legal, Financial, Data) (AA) (2.0)	• Provide easy ways to confirm, correct, or reverse a user action where a mistake would cause a serious real-world consequence (e.g., submitting financial data, entering into a legal agreement, submitting test data, or making a transaction).

International Laws Web Accessibility[5]

Country	Law Name	Law Type
Australia	Disability Discrimination Act 1992	Non-discrimination
Australia	Procurement Standard Guidance	Procurement Recommendation
Canada	Human Rights Act	Non-discrimination
Canada	Policy on Communications and Federal Identity	Mandatory policy
China	Law on the Protection of Persons with Disabilities 1990, as amended	Accessibility law
China	Voluntary Web Accessibility Standard	Recommendation
Denmark	Agreement on the use of open standards for software in the public sector	Mandatory policy
European Union	Web and Mobile Accessibility Directive	Accessibility law
European Union	European Accessibility Act (proposed)	Proposed law
European Union	The European Union's Directive 2016/2012	Accessibility law
Finland	Act on Electronic Services and Communication in the Public Sector	Accessibility law
France	Law N° 2005-102 Article 47	Accessibility law

[5]International Web Accessibility and Policies https://dynomapper.com/blog/27-accessibility-testing/532-international-web-accessibility-laws-and-policies

Country	Law Name	Law Type
France	Order of 29 April 2015 on the general accessibility framework for public administrations	Accessibility law
France	Law N° 2016-1321 Article 106	Digital Governance law
Germany	Act on Equal Opportunities for Disabled Persons of 2002	Non-discrimination law
Germany	Federal Ordinance on Barrier-Free Information Technology	Accessibility policy
Hong Kong	Guidelines on Dissemination of Information through Government Websites	Mandatory policy
India	Rights of Persons with Disabilities Act, 2016 (RPD)	Non-discrimination law
India	Guidelines for Indian Government Websites	Mandatory policy
Ireland	The Disability Act, 2005	Accessibility law
Ireland	Equal Status Acts 2000 to 2004	Non-discrimination law
Ireland	Employment Equality Acts 1998 and 2004	Non-discrimination law
Israel	Equal Rights of Persons with Disabilities Act, as amended	Non-discrimination law
Italy	Law 9 January 2004, n. 4 "Provisions to support the access of disabled people to IT tools" (Stanca Law)	Accessibility law

(continued)

Country	Law Name	Law Type
Japan	Basic Act on the Formation of an Advanced Information and Telecommunications Network Society	Accessibility law
Netherlands	Procurement Law 2012	Procurement law
Netherlands	Policy in the Netherlands	Mandatory policy
New Zealand	Human Rights Act 1993, including amendments	Non-discrimination law
New Zealand	Online Practice Guidelines	Mandatory policy
Norway	Regulations on universal design of ICT	Non-discrimination law
Republic of Korea	Act on Welfare of Persons with Disabilities	Non-discrimination law
Sweden	Discrimination Act (2008:567)	Non-discrimination law
Switzerland	Federal Law on the Elimination of Inequalities for Persons with Disabilities, as amended	Non-discrimination law
Taiwan	Web Accessibility Guidelines 2.0	Mandatory policy
United Kingdom	Equality Act 2010	Non-discrimination law
United States	Section 508 of the US Rehabilitation Act of 1973, as amended	Procurement law, Accessibility law
United States	Americans with Disabilities Act of 1990 (ADA), as amended	Non-discrimination law
United States	Section 504 of the US Rehabilitation Act of 1973, as amended	Non-discrimination law
United States	Section 255 of the Telecommunications Act of 1996	Non-discrimination law

Additional Reading

Designing with Accessibility in Mind

- *A Web for Everyone: Designing Accessible User Experiences* by Sarah Horton

- *Accessibility for Everyone* by Laura Kalbag

- *Accessibility Handbook* by Katie Cunningham

- Accessible UX Principles by Whitney Quesenbery `https://rosenfeldmedia.com/a-web-for-everyone/accessible-ux-principles-and-guidelines/`

- *Just Ask: Integrating Accessibility Throughout Design* by Shawn, Lawton Henry

- *Mismatch: How Inclusion Shapes Design* by Kat Holmes

- *Design Meets Disability* by Graham Pullin

- *Don't Make Me Think, Revisited: A Common Sense Approach to Web Usability* by Steve Krug

- Adobe Accessibility `https://www.adobe.com/accessibility/resources.html`

- Amazon Accessibility for Fire `https://www.amazon.com/gp/feature.html/?&docId=1000632481`

- Accessibility with Microsoft products `https://www.amazon.com/gp/feature.html/?&docId=1000632481`

Development

- ARIA best practices `https://www.w3.org/wiki/PF/ARIA/BestPractices`

- Inclusive Design Patterns - Coding Accessibility Into Web Design by Heydon Pickering

- *Apps for All: Coding Accessible Web Applications,* by Heydon Pickering

- *Responsive Design Workflow (Paperback)* by Stephan Hay

- *Practical Approaches For Designing Accessible Websites* by Smashing Magazine

- *Engineering Software for Accessibility (Developer Reference)* 1st Edition by Microsoft Corporation

- Github Accessibility `https://github.com/collections/web-accessibility`

- Mozilla Accessibility for Developers `https://developer.mozilla.org/en-US/docs/Web/Accessibility`

- Google Accessibility for Developers `https://developers.google.com/web/fundamentals/accessibility/`

Web Content Accessibility Guidelines

- Web Content Accessibility Guidelines 2.0
  https://www.w3.org/TR/WCAG20/

- Web Content Accessibility Guidelines 2.1
  https://www.w3.org/TR/WCAG21/

- WebAIM https://webaim.org

International Resources for Accessibility

- International Association of Accessibility Professionals
  https://www.accessibilityassociation.org

- United Nations Article 9 Accessibility https://
  www.un.org/development/desa/disabilities/
  convention-on-the-rights-of-persons-with-
  disabilities/article-9-accessibility.html

Legal

- *eQuality: The Struggle for Web Accessibility by Persons
  with Cognitive Disabilities (Cambridge Disability Law
  and Policy Series)* by Peter Blanck

- *Making Computers Accessible: Disability Rights and
  Digital Technology* by Elizabeth R. Petrick

- *Structured Negotiation: A Winning Alternative to
  Lawsuits* by Lainey Feingold

Design Principles

- ***Building Design Systems: Unify User Experiences through a Shared Design Language*** by Sarrah Vesselov and Taurie Davis

- Material Design - Accessibility `https://material.io/design/usability/accessibility.html`

- Human Interface Guidelines Accessibility - `https://developer.apple.com/design/human-interface-guidelines/accessibility/overview/introduction/`

User Research

- *Just enough research* by Erika Hall

- *Observing the User Experience: A Practitioner's Guide to User Research* – by Goodman Ph.D. School of Information University of California Berkeley, Elizabeth (Author), Mike Kuniavsky (Author), Andrea Moed (Author)

- *Interviewing Users: How to Uncover Compelling Insights* – by Steve Portigal

- *Validating Product Ideas Through Lean User Research* By Tomer Sharon

- *Handbook of Usability Testing: How to Plan, Design, and Conduct Effective Tests, Second Edition* 2nd Edition by Jeffrey Rubin (Author), Dana Chisnell (Contributor), Jared Spool (Contributor)

- *Universal Methods of Design: 100 Ways to Research Complex Problems, Develop Innovative Ideas, and Design Effective Solutions* – by Bruce Hanington (Author), Bella Martin (Author)

Planning and Implementation

- Planning for Accessibility https://alistapart.com/article/planning-for-accessibility/

- Accessibility Planning and Resource Guide for Cultural Administrators https://www.arts.gov/accessibility/accessibility-resources/publications-checklists/accessibility-planning-and-resource

- Accessibility in Practice https://developer.paciellogroup.com/blog/2014/03/accessibility-practice-process-driven-approach-accessibility/

- Accessibility Prioritization https://www.deque.com/blog/accessibility-prioritization-laying-foundation-strategic-plan/

Usability Testing

- How to Conduct Usability Studies for Accessibility https://www.nngroup.com/reports/how-to-conduct-usability-studies-accessibility/

- Tips for Conducting Usability Studies with Participants with Disabilities https://www.smashingmagazine.com/2018/03/tips-conducting-usability-studies-participants-disabilities/

- Usability and Accessibility: Looking at User Experience through Two Lenses `https://www.usability.gov/get-involved/blog/2013/01/accessibility-and-usability.html`

- Think like an Accessible UX researcher part 3: five common mistakes in usability testing and how to avoid them `https://developer.paciellogroup.com/blog/2019/04/think-like-an-accessible-ux-researcher-part-3/`

- Accessibility Testing Tutorial: What is, Tools & Examples `https://www.guru99.com/accessibility-testing.html`

- Accessibility: Usability for All `https://www.interaction-design.org/literature/article/accessibility-usability-for-all`

Media

- 3Play Media `https://www.nad.org/resources/technology/`

- Federal Social Media Accessibility Toolkit `https://digital.gov/resources/federal-social-media-accessibility-toolkit-hackpad/`

- BBC Future Media Standards and Guidelines `https://www.bbc.co.uk/guidelines/futuremedia/accessibility/`

Web Resources

- a11y Project `https://a11yproject.com`

- a11y Style Guide `https://a11y-style-guide.com/style-guide/`

- Knowability `https://knowbility.org`

- Digital a11y `https://www.digitala11y.com/web-accessibility-resources/`

- 100daysofa11y `https://100daysofa11y.com/category/resources/`

Mixed Realities

- Augmented reality and accessibility `https://www.interaction-design.org/literature/article/accessibility-usability-for-all`

- Able Gamers `https://ablegamers.org/thoughts-on-accessibility-and-vr/`

- Augmented reality and Accessibility W3C `https://www.w3.org/WAI/APA/task-forces/research-questions/wiki/Augmented_Reality_and_Accessibility`

- Accessibility with VR & AR `https://knowbility.org/programs/accessu/2019/accessibility-with-vr-ar/`

- Virtual reality and Accessibility References W#C `https://www.w3.org/WAI/APA/task-forces/research-questions/wiki/Virtual_Reality_and_Accessibility_References`

Voice User Interface

- *Voice User Interface Design* by James P. Giangola, Jennifer Balogh

- *Designing Voice User Interfaces: Principles of Conversational Experiences* 1st Edition by Cathy Pearl

- Tips for Designing Accessibility in Voice User Interfaces https://uxdesign.cc/tips-for-accessibility-in-conversational-interfaces-8e11c58b31f6

- Building Chatbots with Python: Using Natural Language Processing and Machine Learning Paperback – by Sumit Raj

- So you want to be a voice designer https://medium.com/@muppetaphrodite/so-you-want-to-be-a-voice-designer-22cdb3cc5b92

- Designing for Voice https://uxplanet.org/designing-for-voice-c6259f07c49c

- Designing for the future with Voice Prototypes https://uxplanet.org/designing-for-voice-c6259f07c49c

Content and Writing for Accessibility

- *Designing Connected Content: Plan and Model Digital Products for Today and Tomorrow (Voices That Matter)* 1st Edition by Carrie Hane, Mike Atherton

- *Content Strategy for the Web*, 2nd Edition 2nd Edition by Kristina Halvorson, Melissa Rach

- *Ensuring Digital Accessibility through Process and Policy* by Jonathan Lazar, Daniel F. Goldstein, et al.

- Tips for getting started: Writing for Web Accessibility

- 7 Guidelines for writing accessible microcopy `https://blog.prototypr.io/7-guidelines-for-writing-accessible-microcopy-8d52575f5d8e`

- Writing for Accessibility `https://styleguide.mailchimp.com/writing-for-accessibility/`

Accessibility Consultants (The Author does not endorse or recommend products or services. Please do your own research into companies)

- Deque `https://www.deque.com`

- Equal Entry `https://equalentry.com`

- The Carol Center for the Blind `https://carroll.org`

- NFB International Braille and Technology Center for the Blind `https://nfb.org/programs-services/center-excellence-nonvisual-access/international-braille-and-technology-center`

- Knowability `https://knowbility.org`

- Interactive Accessibility `https://interactiveaccessibility.com`

- National Association of the Deaf `https://www.nad.org/resources/technology/`

- Level Access `https://www.levelaccess.com`

- Paciello Group `https://www.paciellogroup.com`

- Tenon `https://tenon.io`

- Web Aim `https://webaim.org`

Disability Organizations

- CSUN (California State University Northridge) `https://www.csun.edu/cod/`

- Disabled List `https://www.disabledlist.org/`

- NFB International Braille and Technology Center for the Blind `https://nfb.org/programs-services/center-excellence-nonvisual-access/international-braille-and-technology-center`

- National Association of the Deaf `https://www.nad.org/resources/technology/`

- Lighthouse `http://lighthouse-sf.org`

Education and Technology

- Association of University Centers on Disabilities: A network of interdisciplinary centers advancing policy and practice for and with individuals with developmental and other disabilities, their families, and communities.

- Center for Applied Special Technology: Advocates for educational products, classroom practices, and products that are inclusive to all.

- National Association of Special Education Teachers: National membership organization dedicated to rendering all possible support and assistance to those preparing for or teaching in the field of special education.

- Assistive Technology Industry Association: A not-for-profit membership organization of manufacturers, sellers, and providers of technology-based assistive devices and services.

- Microsoft Partners in Assistive Technology: Third-party manufacturers of screen readers, magnifiers, and specialty accessibility hardware that are compatible with Microsoft technology.

- The Policy Surveillance Program: The goal of this program is to increase the use of policy surveillance and legal mapping as tools for improving the nation's health. More and more, researchers, policy-makers, public health practitioners, and the media are recognizing the need for access to reliable information about laws and policies that influence the public's health.

- Trace Research and Development Center: Conducts research and advocates for accessibility to new and emerging technologies.

Employment and Business

- Broad Futures: Works to empower young adults with learning disabilities through employment.

- Incight: A nonprofit that aims to eliminate stigma associated with disability and expand inclusion by helping students and jobseekers in particular.

- Partnership on Employment and Accessible Technology: Multifaceted initiative to foster collaboration and action around accessible technology in the workplace. Guided by a consortium of policy and technology leaders, PEAT works to help employers, IT companies, and others to understand why it pays to build and buy accessible technology, and how to do so.

- Our Ability, Building the Business Case for Employment of People with Disabilities: Our Ability consults with businesses to leverage the successful employment of individuals with disabilities.

- US Business Leadership Network: A national nonprofit that unites business around disability inclusion in the workplace, supply chain, and marketplace. More than 130 corporate partners look to USBLN for guidance on disability inclusion, including recruitment and outreach, supplier diversity, and accessibility.

Family and Social Services

- American Association of Caregiving Youth: National resource for children who sacrifice their education, health, well-being, and childhood to provide care for family members who are ill, injured, elderly, or disabled.

- Community Options: Supports people with disabilities through developing residential, employment, and other support services.

- Easter Seals: Founded in 1919, offers therapy, early intervention services, camps and employment placement and helps children and adults with disabilities, caregivers, veterans, and seniors be at their best as they live, learn, work, and play.

- Through the Looking Glass: Pioneers research, training, and services for families in which a child, parent, or grandparent has a disability or medical issue. This nonprofit organization emerged from the independent living movement.

Harassment and Hate Crimes

- All Walks Of Life: Focuses on prevention of violence to people with disabilities with information and a moderated email list.

- US Equal Employment Opportunity Commission: Federal agency that investigates cases of disability discrimination.[6]

---

[6]National Center on Disability Journalism https://ncdj.org/resources/organizations/

Index

X, Y, Z

Printed in the United States
By Bookmasters